THE
HEALING
POWER
OF
Love

Floyd McClung

HARVEST HOUSE PUBLISHERS
Eugene, Oregon 97402

THE HEALING POWER OF LOVE

Copyright © 1995 by Floyd McClung, Jr.
Published by Harvest House Publishers
Eugene, Oregon 97402

Library of Congress Cataloging-in-Publication Data

McClung, Floyd.
     The healing power of love / by Floyd McClung, Jr.
          p.   cm.
     ISBN 1-56507-339-8
     1. Christian life. 2. Spiritual healing. 3. God—Love.
I. Title.
BV4501.2.M2135   1995   95-30156
241'.4—dc20   CIP

Printed in the United States of America.

95 96 97 98 99 00 01 02 — 10 9 8 7 6 5 4 3 2 1

To

David Boyd

Lynn Green

Murray Kilgour

Gordy McDonald

John Goodfellow

Thanks for your friendship, guys!

CONTENTS

1

PAIN AND ITS POWER

*P*ain has terrible power over a person's life—power to control and dominate his or her actions, attitudes, and beliefs. The power of pain is the secret force that motivates most people, even those who see themselves as healthy, "normal" individuals. Psychologists tell us that "pain avoidance" is one of the strongest drives we experience as human beings.

I saw this power clearly at work in the life a young student I met several years ago. Sharon told me she had a boyfriend who was "really bad." She wanted to know if I would help her get out of the relationship. When I asked how she ended up with a guy who was so bad, she told me, "I don't think I'm good enough for the good boys."

"Why do you feel that way?" I asked.

Sharon then told me about her mother. As long as she could remember, every time her mother talked about herself she talked about what a poor mother she was, what a bad person she was, what a failure she was in life. She was a failure in marriage, a failure in work, a failure in school, and a failure to her daughter.

Sharon adopted the same habit of negative confession—so much so that she truly believed she was a bad person. She couldn't stand herself and lived in constant self-hatred. She refused to believe good people would love or accept her; she believed the only people who might accept her were those who were bad. Sharon had not worked out this perception consciously, but she believed it to be true nonetheless.

In her search for a boyfriend, Sharon picked out the biggest problem-maker in school—a young man who always got into fights, got kicked out of class, got drunk, and went in and out of jail. She thought that just maybe this needy young man would love her. She found herself strangely attracted to him and dared to hope that he would not reject her.

Here was a girl living with so much self-image pain that she purposefully moved toward people who were drowning in their own problems—in the anguished, desperate hope that they wouldn't reject her. Sharon tried to deal with her pain by demeaning herself.

Obviously, it didn't work.

Several years ago, my wife Sally and I were counseling a business acquaintance and his wife. They were struggling through some severe marriage problems. The wife's father had been an alcoholic, and silence was his primary means of communication. As a young girl growing up, if she asked permission to do something of which he disapproved, he would simply become silent and refuse to speak a word. Over the years she became supersensitive to her father's nonverbal signals: A look of the eyes. A raised eyebrow. A folding of the arms. These signals all took on enormous weight, far beyond what they might convey in a more stable home.

This woman eventually married the business acquaintance, who happens to have Irish blood. He's outgoing, an extrovert, very expressive. And because she considers everything he does a signal, she has gone through 13 years of hell. All that time she held onto her anger toward her father but never allowed herself to say, "My father failed me. He manipulated me. The way he treated me was unfair." Instead, she has taken out all the pent-up anger on her husband. Her way of describing their marriage relationship is, "My husband, my husband—he's got a problem." She won't allow herself to take any responsibility. To do that would open the door to facing the pain she has not dealt with in her relationship with her father.

My friend, in turn, was not helpful in the way he responded to his wife. He kept saying, "She manipulates me. She won't accept me. She's got a big problem." He, too, refuses to accept responsibility for their problems as a couple.

And now the wife is beginning to drink. One glass of wine has turned into four, then eight, and sometimes ten and twelve a day. All my friend can see is that his wife is turning into an alcoholic, just like her father. When she has dared to open herself up and say, "I'm really hurting. I don't know what's wrong, help me," all he can talk about is her behavior. He cannot see that she is turning to alcohol because of the pain in her life. She can't face what's happening in her marriage, she can't face what happened with her father, and now she's seeking comfort in the bottom of a wine glass.

And so this couple is caught up in a vicious cycle: He criticizes her behavior, she gets hurt and withdraws, so he criticizes her more and makes her hurt worse, and thus the marriage continues its downward spiral. This man and woman have tried to deal with their pain by shifting the blame.

But of course, it's not working.

Some time ago a young woman came to me for counsel. She was a university student, the life of the party, outgoing, fun-loving; she could get everybody around her to laugh and always had a ready joke. Nobody would ever guess what happened when she was alone.

She felt more than lonely, she felt horribly alone, abandoned. Her greatest fear was that people would get close to her only to abandon her. She grew up in a family scarred by patterns of emotional closeness followed by abandonment. More than once her father ran away with other women only to return days or weeks later, begging for forgiveness. She was afraid that would happen to her if she got close to people. She was afraid to believe they would not abandon her.

It was almost as if her outgoing, life-of-the-party personality was a front that kept people at a distance. Nobody would have ever guessed that she was hurting. We spent several tearful sessions in counseling. She was beautiful, she had outstanding leadership abilities, and everyone looked up to her. Yet she was paralyzed by a kind of emotional pain that threatened to swallow her whole.

In one conversation we talked about prayer. She just didn't believe God was listening to her. Oh, on some days she would feel really loved by God. She'd read her Bible, have a quiet time, and feel tremendous. Yet on other days she'd be in quiet agony, wondering if God really did love her, convinced there was something she had done which caused God to abandon her.

One day I sat with her outside at a park bench after a picnic. She sobbed and sobbed. "I am so frightened," she confessed to me through an ocean of tears. "I feel so alone. Nobody knows. I'm afraid to tell people; I'm afraid they'll reject me."

Sharon's fear even affected her relationship with God. She was praying about a new venture in her life, yet was frightened to death of asking God for clear direction. She didn't think He cared enough to talk to her. The pain of rejection was paralyzing her. She tried to deal with it by hiding her pain behind a jovial, outgoing party-girl personality.

But it didn't work.

During the many years I have spent ministering both in the United States and abroad, I have come to one unbending conclusion: If we don't actively look to God for the solution to pain in our life, we will look elsewhere. Uncounted thousands of these "elsewheres" are continuously coming our way, holding out the promise of security, meaning, hope, and comfort.

But none of them work. They never do.

Pain Comes Unlooked For

We don't plan for pain to come into our lives. Neither do we choose it. It can even come to us from well-meaning friends. Ironically, the very person we think might be a real friend often turns out to disappoint us the most.

A short time ago little Joshua Harris found a new friend in front of his grandmother's home in Loveland, Colorado.[1] The 2½-year-old boy reached down to pet a snake and before his grandmother could stop him, the snake uncoiled and fastened its sharp, venomous fangs onto Joshua's bare little arm.

Joshua was raced to a nearby hospital and taken to the intensive care unit, where he received antivenom and was rushed into surgery. Within moments of the strike his arm had swelled up to twice its normal size and his swollen hand had turned green. Had Joshua not received immediate medical attention, he would have died.

That's the way it is with pain. It sneaks up on us and grabs us and bites us. It *hurts*. It can cause us immense suffering and even loss of life if not treated in time.

Pain is horrible and can have unbelievable consequences. Pain can control and dominate our behavior. When we suffer from an emotional wound, the resulting pain—the insecurity or the fear or the shame—can immobilize us and control the way we act. That doesn't mean we have become an absolute prisoner of that pain, but it certainly becomes a dominating force in our life.

Pain can affect what we believe about ourselves. Through pain we begin to believe lies about who we are. The little boy or girl who feels abandoned because of a divorce begins to wonder what he or she has done to cause mommy and daddy to stop loving each other. The adult children of an alcoholic father feel tremendous rage and anger that they seem unable to control or understand. The person struggling in a marriage feels bitterness and begins to interpret these emotions in terms of his or her self-worth, value, or ability to meaningfully contribute to the relationship. Some people begin to see themselves as a failure or even the cause of the problem.

Pain causes some people to seek relief in ways that only furthers their pain. I counseled one woman who, basically, hated men. She attended Bible studies, studied the Word, and expressed concern about spiritual things. But anytime a man crossed her or held her accountable for her actions or words, she became a holy terror. This woman had dominated her husband for years. She was absolutely driven by her fear of men.

She grew up in a rigid church environment; her father was a legalist who dominated her, as were the spiritual leaders in her church. Somehow she took that into her spirit and was deeply wounded by it. She has a deep need for a positive male relationship that can help to heal her fear of men but she won't let any man get close enough to provide the love she so desperately needs.

Millions of people spend their whole lives searching for love and for healing without understanding what drives them. They search desperately for healing but seem unaware that they are being controlled by something.

We Christians are in a spiritual battle with a very real enemy who, on the one hand, inflicts pain—the Bible speaks of Satan as the source of much of the pain that's in our world (*see* John 8:44; 1 Peter 5:8). Yet at the same time he comes to us and offers false alternatives and "escapes" from the very pain he inflicts.

And so it is that pain works its way through our relationships, our beliefs, our attitudes toward God, our trust in Him, how we see the Scriptures, and what we hear people saying or not saying. It seems to permeate our whole life. And if we don't learn God's way of dealing with it, pain will dominate our lives.

Different Kinds of Pain

People experience all kinds of pain. First and most obvious, there's *physical* pain. Physical pain works its way out in relationships. It also affects how the person who is suffering views God. Although this book doesn't focus on physical pain and divine healing, it is important to recognize how dominating physical pain can be. If you've ever stubbed your toe on the foot of your bed, smashed your finger with a hammer, slammed your hand in a car door, or cut yourself with a knife in the kitchen, you know the immediate effects of throbbing, dominating pain.

I can't help but think of my daughter. Right now she is suffering terribly with an excruciating condition known as myalgia encephalomyelitis (also know as fibro myalgia). All of her joints and muscles throb with intense pain. For many months she has known relief only through mind-numbing drugs. Her condition is believed by some doctors to be triggered by a viral illness, and it is aggravated by stress.

She is dealing with the pain as best she can, but there are days when she is simply incapacitated. Whether she wants it to or not, the pain sometimes controls her life. I have agonized over my daughter's condition, not knowing what to do to help her. I want her not to worry, but to tell her that comes across very superficial. She doesn't want the pain, but it is there, hurting her and controlling her.

Misha's pain is a reminder of how dominating pain can be. She experiences physical pain, but her situation is very much like those who suffer from *emotional* pain. Emotional pain can become the center of all a person's thoughts and attention. It can absorb their energy, cause them to lose objectivity, and prompt them to isolate themselves from others.

Lily Tomlin, the comedian, once said, "We're all in this alone." In a way, she's right. Loneliness, abandonment, and shame are unwelcome emotions that plague and overwhelm many of us.

A friend of mine, an Australian, was forced to watch his mother and father held up at gunpoint when he was seven years old. The robber made him tie up his parents. This violent and traumatic episode marked him for life. As a result of the incident, my friend has carried with him a false sense of guilt that he participated in the crime. In actuality, however, he was forced to do this by the thief who broke into their home. His feelings of guilt, then, are not based on his own wrong actions.

Such a sense of false guilt often paralyzes people and forces them to carry an undeserved weight of condemnation. My friend tried to deal with his burden by denying that the incident ever happened; he refused to think about it. This produced in him a kind of emotional deadness. When he shut down his emotions of fear and guilt, all the other emotions shut down as well; he found he couldn't be selective about which emotions he was turning off. He ended up shutting down almost his entire emotional framework. I say *almost* because no one but a corpse is void of all emotions.

The break in my friend's emotional dike came through outbursts of anger. Those of us who thought we knew him were shocked when we witnessed these explosions. He is such a kind man and he really loves his family. He is a great father and husband. But when you got close to him, every once in awhile you'd see for yourself these uncontrolled outbursts of anger. It was only through some friends who pursued him and talked to him, asking questions, that he finally began to open up and face some of his painful feelings.

A third kind of pain is *relationship* pain. Disappointment and hurt in relationships is probably one of the greatest sources of pain we deal with.

Sugar Ray Leonard, the boxer, was speaking at Harvard University. "I consider myself blessed," he told the audience. "You're blessed, we're all blessed. We've

all been blessed with God-given talents. Mine just happens to be beating people up."

I guess some people believe that is their calling in life—they go through life beating up others. Then there are those who don't seem happy unless they get themselves into a relationship in which somebody is beating up on *them*. Whatever psychological terms we might use to describe such relationships, they're definitely unhealthy.

Still others of us have a hard time facing the fact that sometimes *we* are the ones who cause pain in our relationships. I don't like to think of myself as someone who hurts the people I love the most, but it does happen.

Several weeks before Christmas one year, my wife Sally and I were traveling together on a well-deserved break. She wanted to tell me about some issues confronting her. I felt threatened by what she said and became very defensive. This immediately stopped the communication. Sally told me she felt as if I weren't listening to her—that I wasn't taking her seriously and that I wasn't open to hearing her. (All of which was true!) I didn't *want* to hear her because I thought she was accusing me of being the cause of her problems.

Later, when I took time to think about it, I realized I was overreacting. I finally admitted to myself that I was not giving my wife the freedom to share with me some of her struggles. As I worked this through, I finally realized she was not trying to blame me for anything; she was just trying to say, "Floyd, this is what I'm struggling with." Yet it was very hurtful for her that

I refused to listen to her. She felt cut off and injured because the one person closest to her didn't seem to want to help her through her problem. To use biblical language, she felt I didn't want to "bear her burden."

As I write this I'm also struggling in a relationship with a close friend. It seems as if every time we talk to each other, more hurt or confusion results. Our words are not helping us right now; they only lead to more misunderstanding. We're both committed to each other and to working through our difficulty, yet our current predicament is one more example of how even close friends can hurt each other. Relationship pain is so real and intense and has the potential to affect us very deeply.

Emotional Walls and Bitter Roots

As bad as pain can be, unresolved pain is far worse. Among other consequences, pain left unresolved can cause us to raise walls between ourselves and others.

A young woman once asked Sally and I to give her some counsel. Yet it seemed as though this young woman raised an emotional brick wall whenever we began asking questions. Her answers became increasingly vague and nebulous. An empty look came over her face, her speech became monotone, and her eyes grew flat and dead. I finally asked her, "Are you purposefully hiding your pain from us? Is there some problem you're hiding that you don't want to talk about?" She looked at me and coolly stated, "I made a promise to myself when I was 16 years old. A friend hurt me and betrayed my confidence, and I decided right then that I would

20

never let anyone get close enough to hurt me like that again."

Pain not only makes us tentative about relationships and raises walls between us and others, it also makes us susceptible to bitterness. Emotional pain, unless dealt with properly, turns into a festering wound—just as the finger that's slammed in the door or hit by the hammer, if not treated properly, will become infected. Such infections can have serious consequences. This "root of bitterness" will become the source of many other problems in our life. It will manifest itself through harshness, a critical attitude, withdrawal, revenge, hatred, broken relationships, mistrust, suspicion, and a host of other hostile emotions. These problems develop and grow when we refuse to face and properly deal with the hurt that comes into our life.

Some people become slaves of their pain. Bitterness, hatred, or a lack of forgiveness becomes the most powerful force in their life. The simple fact that they refuse to deal with it *in the way that they should* imprisons them behind walls of fear and suspicion and enslaves them to their own hatred and bitterness. They see every person, every relationship, every situation, through tainted glasses—through the bars of the prison cell they've created around themselves.

But it doesn't have to be that way!

No One Is Immune to Pain

Before I begin to suggest how to bring healing to our pain, it's important to recognize that painless people are not real. Anybody who is emotionally one-dimensional, who has allowed themselves to be deadened or desensitized to some dimension of pain in their own life, seems not to be a whole person. They're not "here," so to speak. They certainly are not *there* for you when you need them.

Every normal person experiences emotional pain at one time or another. It can come in the form of disappointment in a relationship, through a feeling of betrayal from a friend who has let us down or shared a secret, or via criticism or an attack upon our personality or character. It can come in business, it can come at home, it can come through school or church or clubs. Those who are closest to us and whom we love the most are often the ones who cause us the greatest pain. To the degree that you love deeply, you feel deeply about a person. And to that degree the person can hurt you.

So what is the answer to such pain? Is there a solution? All of us have pain; the question is, how do we deal with it?

Where Do We Go from Here?

Personal problems can be excruciating to face, especially when laced with emotional pain. Yet a wound that goes untended, like a cancer that goes undealt with, can quietly spread through our body. We may hate to go to doctors or to dentists for fear of the bad news they may bring, but avoiding the problem doesn't make it go away. Though lancing a wound or pulling a bad tooth is hurtful in the beginning, it's a necessary step toward healing. We are not going to know relief until we face our pain and admit, "I have a problem. I need help. I'm hurting."

The same is true of our *emotional* woundedness—the pain we feel, the insecurities, and the fear that chokes us. Failure to deal with the pain won't make our condition improve.

Consider the university student who spends hours before a mirror trying to look glamorous. She spends herself in frantic efforts to appear attractive and sexy—yet never seems to be satisfied no matter how many young men express interest in her. Or think of the young professional woman who's seemingly secure—but at the same time is cutting in her remarks, even mean, with a real edge to her personality. Or observe the businessman who appears extremely successful. He drives a BMW, has a boat, enjoys a place at the beach and travels around Europe for vacations—but underneath is a striving, driven man who is failing as a father and a husband. These are real-life examples, all of them. I know each of these people personally.

In each case, events have helped to affect the behavior of these people and shape what they believe about themselves.

The university student believes she is not as pretty as the other women around her. She is driven to be beautiful, but can't see herself that way. The young professional woman was raised by a lesbian mother who goaded her into developing negative patterns of coping. To this day she doesn't realize these behavior patterns are putting off her friends and sending people away. The businessman was abandoned as a child by an alcoholic father and decided way back then that he was not going to be like his dad. Instead, he was going to be an overcomer. That became the driving, controlling force of his life.

Maybe your own story is similar to one of those I've just recounted. Or perhaps it's nothing like any of them. Yet all of us carry emotional baggage that affects how we see ourselves and how we behave. Some of us have grown accustomed to our wounds and to the behavior that grows out of those wounds. We think it is normal. We operate like the fortune teller who studied the hand of a young man and said to him, "You will be poor and unhappy and your life will be filled with pain until you are 37 years old." "After that, what will happen?" asked the anxious young man. "You will still be poor and unhappy and filled with pain, but you'll get used to it," she replied.

Some people are like that; they resign themselves to a pain-filled existence and tell themselves it's just their cross to bear. Most of us, however, aren't like that at all. We *never* get used to pain. We feel our pain very deeply. Our problem is that we just don't know how to get rid of it.

Whether we are conscious or unconscious of our pain, we all fall into a common pattern: avoid it at all costs! That's only natural. God didn't create us to live with pain. So we avoid it—and we seek some form of pleasure to alleviate the pain. We do so by driving ourselves to succeed, through our perfectionism, by controlling people around us, by attacking those who hurt us, by withdrawing, and by a thousand other faulty avoidance and coping mechanisms.

God did not create us to bear the emotional weight of shame, guilt, fear, or anger. God never intended for these emotions to be a part of our lives. So when we experience them, if we don't deal with them God's way—in the way that He has provided—we will end up trying to cope with them in ways that never truly resolve the problem.

This book has been written not only to expose some of the faulty schemes for dealing with pain, but much more to sketch out what I have called *the healing power of love*. We *can* deal with our pain in the way God wants us to, and thereby get beyond that pain and become the kind of healthy, productive, life-affirming men and women that we all desire to be.

When I sat down to write this book, I had at least four purposes in mind. Use the following list as a sort of road map for what follows in the rest of the book. I wrote *The Healing Power of Love:*

1. To help us understand pain and its power to control our attitudes and behavior;

2. To help us recognize how we respond to unresolved hurts and fears, and to identify how we try to deny or escape our pain through what I call the false ways of healing;

3. To enable us to recognize and receive God's true healing love;

4. To equip us to help other people receive God's healing love.

In the next chapter I want to begin our journey by talking about the ways that all of us try to avoid pain, and how our efforts can either encourage or short-circuit the healing God wants to bring to us.

Along these lines, I'm reminded of something Charlie Brown once said to his friend Lucy: "There is no problem so big that I can't run away from it."

In real life, acting on Charlie's proverb is a sure recipe for more pain.

2

IF IT'S PAIN, I DON'T WANT IT!

*T*wo men were talking. One was huge, handsome, muscular; the other was puny, homely, and always felt insignificant. The small man wanted to be big so he could impress people. He was admiring the size of the big fellow and said to him, "If I were as big as you, I wouldn't be afraid of nuthin'. I'd go out and find me the biggest bear in the woods and I'd tear him from limb to limb." The big man looked down at his diminutive admirer and replied, "Well, there are a lot of little bears in the woods."

Moral: Whether our problems are big or little, when they're *our* problems, they're big!

I spend a lot of time hiking in the mountains of Colorado. Last October I was on a camping trip with my son in the Sangre de Cristo mountains of Southern Colorado. We camped out for three nights in a lonely meadow on the side of a mountain. One day we decided to explore a dense patch of woods on one side of the valley we were camping in. As we were hiking along a narrow animal trail we came upon what were obviously fresh bear tracks. We followed the tracks for about three hours when we arrived at the bear's den.

To be honest, I had mixed feelings about following those tracks—especially when we came to the spot where the tracks disappeared over an embankment. It was exciting, but there was just enough possibility of danger to make me concerned about what would happen if we stumbled on ol' sawtooth himself. To investigate the bear's den, I hung onto a tree while I leaned over the ledge. Then, to impress my 20-year-old son that I was a brave woodsman, I decided to walk down the ledge and get a better look at the den. Although snow covered the ground and I thought there was a good chance the animal had already gone into hibernation, I was not sure what would happen when I looked into that hole in the side of the mountain.

The problems we encounter in life are much the same way. We know we should face them; we want to face them; we even want to impress other people by showing that we are willing to face them. But when we think about coming face-to-face with those toothy difficulties, we're not sure we really want to confront them, right?

The bear we had been following had grown to huge proportions in my imagination by the time we came upon his den. Nor did it help to know that we lived in an area of the Colorado mountains where there is a large bear population. I had personally sighted about 40 bears the previous spring, some of them scrounging through the trash cans outside my back door. Although the bear den turned out to be empty, the rush of adrenaline I experienced when I looked into that bear den was very real. It turned out that I didn't need to be afraid, but that didn't change my feelings!

A Basic Drive

Although I am 6' 6" and weigh more than 250 pounds, I have to admit that I don't like pain any more than I like the idea of getting mixed up in a bear fight. Just like the bear we were tracking, the idea of finding what is causing my pain is enough to make me ignore my aches and pains for as long as possible. My wife, who is only 5' 6" and less than half my weight, sometimes accuses me of being a "pain coward." Years ago when we were living in Afghanistan I came down with amoebic dysentery and was suffering from terrible stomach cramps. My wife stood over me and insisted that my condition was nowhere near as painful as childbirth. "Get up," she chastised me. Meanwhile, I continued to insist that I was about to die and pled for a doctor to come immediately. As I said earlier, I don't like pain!

Pain avoidance is one of the most basic drives of our human nature. To a certain degree, that's understandable. When a child touches a burning stove, it hurts, and we teach the child not to put his or her hand on the hot stove again. When a child runs into the street to play and is struck by a car, the incident becomes a lifelong lesson (if the child isn't killed). We become cautious when we are hurt physically, and the same is true when we are hurt emotionally.

God has created us with the ability to experience physical and emotional pain. We're designed in such a way that we know we should avoid pain and its source. Yet at the same time, if emotional pain *does* exist in our life, refusing to face it will only worsen the pain.

Two Ways of Avoiding Pain

If we refuse to face our pain, we'll generally do one of two things: we'll either run from it or cover it up. Either we will withdraw, hide, deny; or we will act compulsively in a frenzied effort to mask the pain.

These withdrawal and compulsion patterns explain a lot about human behavior. We can see them all the way back to the Garden of Eden. When Adam and Eve sinned and God came to walk with them in the garden, they responded in these two ways. They ran away (withdrawal), and they stitched together fig leaves to cover themselves (compulsion). One is a defense mechanism; the other is a comfort mechanism.

Compulsion generally manifests itself in comfort patterns and sensory appeasal—that is, eating, alcohol, drugs, sex, and dependent relationships. Some people will work long hours or do anything they can to find acceptance or achieve success. These people have a compelling desire to be in control of everyone and everything they relate to. They can also be perfectionists. If a job is not done just right, or if they aren't dressed perfectly, then they do more and work harder to achieve the acceptance or control they crave. Pity the person who gets in their way!

Robert McGee says in his excellent book *The Search for Significance,* "Whoever doesn't contribute to their success and acclaim is a threat to their self-esteem—an unacceptable threat. They may be very personable and have lots of 'friends,' but the goal of these relationships may not be to give encouragement and love; it may be to manipulate others to contribute to their success. That may sound harsh, but people who are driven to succeed will often use practically everything and everybody to meet that need."[1]

The other category of behavior in response to pain is *withdrawal,* which is characterized by attempts to avoid failure and disapproval by hiding from situations or people that are threatening to us. The fear of rejection and the desire to avoid any situation that brings more pain or recurrence of pain motivates the behavior of the person who withdraws. He or she wants to be around people who will accept or comfort, not someone who will cause more pain.

A person who withdraws tends to avoid or attack relationships that demand emotional vulnerability or that confront him with unresolved emotional pain. Such a person can develop elaborate walls in his personality, including super-spirituality, that keep him out of the hurt and pain of his past. He may appear to be godly or easygoing, but in fact he is running from anyone or anything that threatens his emotional equilibrium.

Most of us exhibit some combination of these two behaviors. We're willing to step out, take risks, and do things when we feel secure or assured of acceptance. But we avoid people or circumstances that might bring us pain.

Whatever You Call It, It's Flesh

The Bible calls both of these avoidance patterns "the flesh." Everything we do apart from genuine dependence on Christ to avoid pain falls into one of these two patterns in life. Both of them, though they can look good on the outside, are merely different ways of avoiding pain.

The apostle Paul used the word *flesh* in several different ways. By looking at his letter to the Romans we can see one of the primary ways he defined the flesh. In that epistle he is trying to show two warring parties, the Jews and the Gentiles, how the flesh affects those who believe in Christ. He says that as long as the Jews are dependent upon the law and the Gentiles are dependent upon indulgence of their desires, they are both *in the flesh*. One is a religious type of flesh; the other is a nonreligious type. One tries to earn God's acceptance, the other revels in self-gratification. But they're both flesh.

In Paul's mind, *anything that is not an expression of total dependence upon Christ is an act of the flesh—an attempt to avoid what Christ has done for us on the cross.*

We see the same lesson in Galatians. It's my theory that the Galatian Christians were once pagans.² Paul led them out of idolatry to a vital knowledge of Christ. But after Paul left the scene, false teachers came along and said something like, "You heard the gospel through

Paul. How's it going? Have you had any problems since Paul left? Are you still struggling with some areas of sin in your life? You are? That fits the pattern. *All* of Paul's converts go through this! They struggle to have victory. Do you know why? It's because Paul didn't tell you the whole gospel. Not only do you have to believe in Jesus, but you also need to obey the law."

Paul soon hears about this subversion and he's furious as he sets pen to paper. He says to the Galatians, "Having begun by the Spirit, are you now being perfected by the flesh?" (Galatians 3:3 NASB). These people started in idolatry, they were set free in grace, and then they returned to idolatry—only this time, a religious form of idolatry. Paul compares these two forms of flesh when he writes about the law in chapters 2 and 3 of Galatians, and about giving into the flesh in chapters 5 and 6 of his letter. The Galatians had experienced both forms of flesh.

My point is this: Whether we seek freedom from pain through religion or through satisfying our passions and desires, our efforts won't work. The Bible calls both methods flesh because they're a substitute for the way God has provided to set us free from the flesh.

Anything we do to avoid pain, stress, broken relationships, and conflict with other believers—anything other than going to Jesus—is the flesh. It can be a religious form of flesh or it can be a sensual form. It can be withdrawal or compulsion, but it is still the flesh. Whatever it is, if we are not taking everything to Christ and resolving our negative emotions, our pain, and dealing with our sin and the sin of others against us in the way that God has shown and provided for us, we will end up in the flesh. It is inevitable.

It is even possible for us to change our outward behavior but inwardly still not trust in Christ. *Behavior alone is not the issue.* There are many people who take on religious behavior or change the way they perform, but their motivation is still to impress people, prove their worth, or gain acceptance. They want to find their identity in what they are *doing.* All this is done in contrast to trusting Christ for forgiveness, for acceptance, and for our identity. Let me say it again: *Anything that we put our trust in other than Christ is an act of the flesh. Anything.*

People from both good and bad families, functional and dysfunctional families, develop flesh patterns. We can see a biblical example of this in the story of the prodigal son. Two sons responded in different ways to the same father. Some people are like the prodigal himself, who ran and tried to escape from his problems. Others are like the older brother, who stayed home and put his trust in his deeds. The Bible says that if we trust in our religious deeds or deny our problems and run from them, we are acting in the flesh.

There is a basic lie at the root of both religious and nonreligious flesh-patterns. That lie is that we will find our significance or forgiveness or overcome guilt or fear or shame or find importance in something we do or don't do. The truth, however, is that we will find our healing only in the love of Jesus. But we're getting ahead of ourselves.

The problem with trying to avoid pain through withdrawal or compulsion is that these patterns have their roots in an emotional seedbed of fear, shame, guilt, and anger. While God planted the Tree of Life in the Garden of Eden, all too often our lives are a tree of death that grows out of the soil of unresolved emotional pain. Unfortunately, this tree bears fruit that is inconsistent with our desire to bring glory to God. We want to please Him, but we cannot because of the unresolved pain in our lives.

Let's focus for a moment on four soul-killing emotions found within us. My basic premise is that these four emotions are common to all people and that they are a result either of our own sin or the sin of others against us. Regardless, these emotions lead to behavior and attitudes that are the fruit of not dealing with them the way we should: facing them head on and rooting them out of our lives by acknowledging their presence, taking responsibility for them, forgiving those who have contributed to their existence in our lives, and repentance.

Four Soul-Killing Emotions

1. *Shame*

Shame is a feeling of hopelessness that we cannot change—that there is no alternative for us. It's connected to our personhood and is related directly to our self-esteem. It causes us to think, *That's the way I am. I can't change. I'll always be like this.*

Shame leads to feelings of passivity, self-pity, destructive behavior, feelings of inferiority, withdrawal, anger toward others, loss of creativity, and unhealthy dependence on certain people. Those people who experience shame struggle with hopelessness; they feel that they are worthless, that they are a failure. They wrestle with feelings of condemnation and abandonment and are often driven with a desire to punish others because of how bad they feel about themselves. The person struggling with shame can be manipulative; he will do to others what has been done to him. He will make demands and manipulate people in an attempt to control their behavior. This is called shame-based behavior.

If we base our self-worth on past experiences—especially negative experiences during which other people put us down or make demands of us—our self-image will become attached in an unhealthy manner to a permeating sense of failure and shame. In fact, shame-based people tend to excuse their actions with an attitude of hopelessness; the result is that they permanently identify themselves as failures. Deep within themselves they may have unresolved anger in response to a parent who helped produce the shame they feel, but they express this anger by treating other people the same way they were treated: manipulating and demanding more.

I was counseling a couple last Monday night. The husband is a hardworking businessman; he is a goal-oriented entrepreneur. But in his heart he struggles with self-righteous anger. The wife is an extraordinarily sensitive person. She's one of the most hospitable, gracious, romantic women I know.

The previous week, this couple had a bad argument. During a three-hour fight, he blew her away. "It's finished," the wife told me. "It won't work. It's hopeless."

"Listen," I said to him. "God put you together with this wonderful woman. You desperately need her and yet you're wounding her every time you open your mouth."

My friend responded by pouting. "I just never can please her," he moaned.

"Now, wait a minute," I said. "Either you blew it or you didn't. Either you sinned or you didn't; there is no middle ground here. If you were harsh and angry with her, you're guilty. If you're guilty, you ought to look your wife in the eye and say, 'I sinned.' But don't pout!"

My friend was wallowing in shame, in condemnation, in his "poor me" routine—which was robbing him of good, healthy conviction. Most of us will agree that we are "totally depraved" in the theological sense, but when it comes right down to it, we don't like to think of ourselves as all that bad. Oh, we've got problems and Jesus went to the cross for those problems, but we're not desperate sinners; our hearts are not as dark as night.

Condemnation robs us of conviction and leaves us with something that's half-baked: a feeling of shame and worthlessness. God-inspired conviction is intended to lead to a profound repentance that motivates a positive change in our behavior—not a vague feeling of personal worthlessness. Paul wrote, "Godly sorrow brings repentance that leads to salvation and leaves no regret, but worldly sorrow brings death" (2 Corinthians 7:10).

Shame can be a healthy emotion when it's prompted by real guilt for real sin, but when it is a constant nagging feeling of failure—a cloud hanging over you that makes you think *I'm no good*—it can produce a terrible pattern of denial about your responsibility for your sin against others, and leave you feeling responsible for what in reality is the consequence of someone else's sin against you. Shame tempts us sorely to not take ownership for what we do to hurt people in response to their sin against us, and thus we perpetuate the vicious cycle that started with a parent or close authority figure doing the same to us. Even though shame is rooted in what others have done to us, the power of shame will be broken only when we ask for and receive from God a revelation of our own fleshly manipulation of the people in our life...and a revelation of His great love and acceptance of us as His dear children.

I've seen this in my relationship with Sally. If we have an argument and I carry a sense of failure for my part of the argument, it usually will tempt me to not deal honestly with my part of the conflict. By the way, *for those of us who have been abused in the past, it is especially difficult for us to own up to responsibility in our sin because it feels like the put-down feeling we had when we were abused or manipulated.*

I have known young people who were manipulated by "religious" parents. Their parents would communicate in a condemning way to put them down and control their behavior. Many of these young people often end up with a shame-based personality. Some ended up hating religion or God. Others ended up treating people the same way they had been treated. Still others carried a lot of unresolved anger and hostility.

Most people with shame-based personalities cannot think about the past without feeling a sense of failure. They are dominated by a sense of rejection from their parents. They cannot recall their past without experiencing strong, painful emotions. They feel certain experiences have come close to ruining them. They feel they have lost opportunities to experience a complete life.

That's why I felt I had to confront my pouting friend and say, "Either you blew it or you didn't." It helped him because he was in that middle ground, saying, "Oh, I can never please her" and, "Yeah, I blew it again" and, "Isn't God ever satisfied?" As I listened to him, I thought, *That's not conviction. He's dealing with this superficially. His wife is devastated; she said he was really angry and that it's an ongoing problem. So either he is wrong or right.* When I confronted him with those thoughts, he opened up. He started talking about how his father had treated him as a young teenager, browbeating him and mocking his best efforts. When I described shame as a dominating emotion that kills our soul, he acknowledged for the first time that he felt shame often. It was hard for him to admit these feelings as a man, but he did.

It is only when we recognize the power of shame as a motivating emotion that we can begin to deal with real guilt without feeling that we are compromising ourselves. We are then free to come to God and say, "Guilty." And it is then that we can really hear for the first time, "Forgiven." The singer Michael Card said much the same thing in one of his most poignant lyrics: "We look into our Judge's eyes and find a Savior there."

This is God's answer to shame: He adopts us into His family and frees us from the power of shame. He chooses us and then puts His Spirit within us to convince and confirm to us that we are wanted. The Spirit of God bears witness with our spirit that we are loved and wanted (*see* Romans 8:16). In that way, the painful emotion of shame is lifted off of us.

2. Guilt

The unresolved emotion of guilt can result in tremendous fear, alienation, and confusion. Some people respond to guilt like a dog that's been repeatedly beaten by its owner. They feel put down and worthless. Others deal with guilt through what Robert McGee calls the "numbing effects of denial."[3]

There is both true and false guilt. True guilt is the conviction we receive from the Holy Spirit when we have broken one of God's laws. False guilt is imposed by others. It is guilt that comes from people around us who impose standards or rules that have nothing to do with sin. These imposed rules and social restraints have nothing to do with how God has designed for us to live or what God designed us to avoid. False guilt is what we feel when we're afraid of losing the love of others. True guilt is a fact; false guilt is a feeling of pain or condemnation.

The emotion of guilt, whether false or true, leads to the lie, "I must avoid failure." Guilt-driven people are performers. They feel that they must atone for their failures; they must overcome their weaknesses and show they are OK. "I must get God or others to approve of me."

No emotion can be so paralyzing or destructive as false guilt. It causes a loss of self-respect, it undermines confidence, it causes the human spirit to wither and die, and it eats away at our self-worth.

Before coming to Christ, we stand guilty before God because of our rebellion against Him. After coming to Christ, if we continue to feel that sense of guilt even though God has accepted us, we are suffering from false guilt. Such false guilt leads to shame or condemnation—to a vague sense of failure without any specific knowledge of what wrong we have done.

This is God's answer to guilt: He has taken the guilt of our sin upon Himself and carried it to the cross. He died and took the punishment we deserve. He stood in our place and took our punishment to free us from guilt. That may seem almost too good to be true, but it is.

What would motivate God to do that? Immense, infinite love and never-ending mercy. He created us for a relationship with Him and even though we sinned against Him, He responded to us with love by sending His Son Jesus to die for us. We could summarize what God did in this way: The Creator created us for a relationship, and we rebelled against His loving and reasonable laws. Then the Creator sent His Son in the form of a creature to reach out to us. We crucified the Creator's Son on the cross, rejecting the Creator's offer of pardon and friendship. Then the Creator used this ultimate act of selfishness—crucifying His Son—to be the source of our forgiveness. He turned the act of our ultimate rejection into one more offer of pardon and reconciliation! What do you do with such love? Either you acknowledge your guilt and accept the offer of pardon, or you deny your sin and continue in your guilt-producing ways.

The very same offer of pardon for true guilt is the same solution for false guilt, with just one difference: God makes it clear to us that the false guilt is exactly that. There are rules that are not His rules. There are imposed regulations and religious expectations that have nothing to do with God. His Word makes that clear. While removing our real guilt He also offers to remove the vague sense of condemnation and false guilt: "Therefore, there is now no condemnation for those who are in Christ Jesus, because through Christ Jesus the law of the Spirit of life set me free from the law of sin and death" (Romans 8:1-2).

3. *Anger*

Anger is an inner sense of bitterness, hatred, or hostility toward a person for the wrong he or she has done to us. Anger is often unconscious and can explode unexpectedly. It can build up like a lake behind a dam and burst out when the pressure exceeds the dam's limit.

Anger is often a person's response to rejection or abandonment and usually includes a desire to get even. Anger comes because a person has not understood how deeply he feels about rejection, abandonment, or being misunderstood. It builds up within a person because he has not allowed himself to deal honestly with how he feels he was treated.

Anger also comes from a fear of punishment. If a person feels he can't live up to the expectations of another and that he will be punished as a result, he may try to defend himself by lashing out toward others. Anger leads to self-induced punishment, bitterness, revenge, and hatred.

On the cross, Jesus dealt with anger by taking our fears, punishment, abandonment, and rejection. He bore all those upon Himself. He took upon His own person all that is evil and unclean and unrighteous so that we could be free. We can give Him all that is in our hearts and let Him take the anger away. He has given us a new heart where the fear of punishment is gone and the certainty that we are loved and wanted is accepted as the rule of the day.

God has given us another way of dealing with anger: He allows us the freedom to tell Him honestly how we feel—to express our anger to him in private without fear of rejection or retribution. *You can do that!*

That truth has liberated me. I came to realize I would not shock God if I told Him exactly how I felt about someone. I found out He *wanted* me to do that! I was amazed that He invited me to be so honest with Him. I found it liberating just to express my hurt or disappointment to Him about others, and sometimes about Him, and then to let the resulting hostility be poured out in honest and sometimes emotional prayer.

Of course, it is important that we don't stop there. God is not the great shrink in the sky, the all-passive therapist who only wants to listen. He also invites us (an "invitation that cannot be turned down!") to go beyond the anger we feel to ask His help in forgiving or accepting those who have hurt or disappointed us. What's amazing is that He listens to our anger and then loves us unconditionally! He helps us forgive the people we are angry at.

4. Fear

Fear is conceived in the human heart in many ways. It can come through rejection, abandonment, abuse, legalism, or noncommunication. Fear can result from unintended offenses, the little things a person close to us says or does that hit us the wrong way. Fear can also result from an accident or a traumatic event in our life that marks us emotionally. Fear can also come through sexual or verbal abuse. Exposure to authoritarian leadership can cause us to lose our confidence and feel fear.

There are normal fears, of course: the fear of the unknown, the fear of heights, the fear of death, the fear of fire. But then there is an extreme kind of fear: the fear that cripples a person, the fear that robs him of his ability to function with confidence and joy. Some people have unusual fears like arachnophobia (fear of spiders) or agoraphobia (fear of open spaces) or a thousand other fears with unpronounceable names.

Fear cripples us when it causes us to start believing false things. Our fears can become like a darkroom where all the images that lurk undeveloped or invisible within us get processed into four-color prints. Our imagination runs away with us and everything that we feared would happen to us becomes a reality in our minds.

I had a friend who, when she was a child, was thrown into the deep end of a swimming pool to "teach her to swim." When she floundered and became frightened, she was mocked and ridiculed. The trauma put such tremendous fear in her heart that she still struggles to overcome that fear today.

Fear will lead us to do anything we can to avoid rejection and gain approval. To find value and love, we will take vows like, "I'm not going to let anyone get close enough to hurt me." No way am I going to get close to people who criticize me. Forget that."

Pain and fear go hand in hand, whether we're talking about emotional or relational pain. We're afraid to be hurt again like we have been in other relationships. We are afraid of losing control. We are afraid of the unknown. We are afraid of what we might be asked to do or forced to do if we confront our pain or the person who caused that pain. We are afraid of suffering and continuing to suffer.

Fear of rejection is one of the greatest fears of all, and rightfully so. Though at times it can be an imaginary fear, once a person has experienced rejection, he is not likely to expose himself to situations that could lead to rejection again. I myself am a big guy and I am very confident in myself, but there are some people and situations that I have decided I just don't want to be around. I am afraid of what those people will do. I am not physically afraid of them, but it has been my experience that after I have been around them I feel disappointed, hurt, or confused. And I don't like being hurt! I have struggled and wondered how I should respond to these people. I have asked God to help me respond in the right way, but meanwhile I don't expose myself to further hurt unless the Lord gives me direction to reach out to them, and I have faith in my heart to do that.

I know that because of what Jesus accomplished on the cross and because of what He made possible—our adoption into God's family, our new status as the permanent residence of the Holy Spirit—we no longer have to let fear control us. I have achieved victory in many of the relationships that once brought fear into my life, and in some other relationships I am still trusting God to give me victory.

I believe what the Word says: "There is no fear in love. But perfect love drives out fear, because fear has to do with punishment. The one who fears is not made perfect in love" (1 John 4:18). Thank God there is hope in overcoming our fears!

Responding to the Four Soul-Killing Emotions

Not only do we try to avoid our pain, but it is in those very "pain avoidance mechanisms" that we try to find our security and value.

So what can we do?

+ We all have pain;

+ Different people have different thresholds for emotional pain, but *everyone* has experienced pain no matter how much they can tolerate it before they respond to it;

✦ However great our tolerance for pain, it eventually affects our behavior and our attitudes;

✦ We're not created to bear the deep emotions of shame, guilt, anger, and fear;

✦ If we don't take the four soul-killing emotions to God, we will go someplace else to deal with them, whether we withdraw or seek comfort to escape their hurtful presence.

Does God really care about our pain? Or must we bear it alone? Where can we take our pain to be healed—truly healed? And what do we do about the scars left behind . . . the attitudes and behavior that develop as part of our responses to pain? In moments of honesty we all realize at one time or another that through withdrawal from pain or through seeking comfort to escape pain, certain behavior develops in our lives that causes other people pain. What, then, can we do?

Redeeming Our Pain

The French painter Renoir suffered excruciating pain from rheumatoid arthritis. When asked why he continued to paint when the arthritis made it torture for him to move his hand, his answer revealed his heart. He said, "The pain passes, but the beauty remains."[4]

So it is with pain that we face with God's help. God can help you face your pain and be free from it.

But He does more than just take it away. He turns our emotional scars and painful experiences into beautiful reminders of victory.

I have an acquaintance from Kansas City. As a young man he ran from the call of God upon his life. While he was living in rebellion and flaunting an ungodly lifestyle, he suffered a terrible accident. Working to repair a high voltage line, his ladder slipped and he instinctively reached out and grabbed the live wire. Instantly his entire body was burned horribly. His injury was so severe no one at the hospital thought he would live.

The boy's father, a minister, came to the hospital to visit his son every day. During that difficult time of recuperation my friend began to face the fact that running from God was a far greater problem in his life than the burns that covered his body. "If I lost my life," he asked himself, "what would I have gained?" The answer, he realized, was nothing.

So right there in the hospital he asked the Lord to give back his life and give him the opportunity to serve Him. Today, as a minister of the gospel, the only scar that remains on his body after many operations is on the back of one hand. He told me once that every time he stands to preach, he's glad for that scar. It's a reminder to him of the grace of God in his life.

God can turn our scars into reminders of His deeper work of transforming us, of freeing us. They point us back to a time when God was busy redeeming the pain that threatened to engulf us, and point us forward to a confident reliance on the further grace that He longs to pour upon us.

Scars also do something else. They serve as a permanent memorial to the reality of pain. Long after the intense emotion of the pain has subsided, the scar remains to wordlessly testify of an agony gone by. In a sense, it is God's way of saying, "I take your pain seriously. I know that you are hurting and I am working to bring about your healing. I take you seriously and I take your emotions seriously. You are, after all, my precious child."

You see, God doesn't demean your emotions brought out by painful experiences. He doesn't disregard them. And He doesn't ask you to disregard them. When you hurt, God cares. He sees your pain and reaches out to you to free you from its torturous presence. But that involves the difficult process of facing the hurt so that we can be free . . . so that we can be healed by God's love.

It also means allowing God to put the plow of His Spirit into the ground of our hearts and dig up those painful emotions. The four soul-killers of shame, fear, anger, and guilt are like seeds in our hearts. They must be dug out or they will grow into trees that produce ungodly fruit—flesh patterns that will control and eventually destroy us.

We can trust God to help us face our pain because He has also experienced pain. We can face our pain because He enables and comforts us as one who suffers with us. The nail prints in His hands forever remind us that God deeply cares—that He too has suffered and so He understands. But He not only understands, He also frees our emotions so we might feel without fear . . . that we might hope and laugh and cry again.

3

SETTING OUR
FEELINGS FREE

I *happened to be visiting my psychologist cousin when*
he returned home after a long flight. For the second
or third time in a row, the airlines had lost his luggage.
He was angry. I couldn't help but think, It's going to be
interesting to see how a psychologist handles anger.

He walked in the room, sat down deliberately on the couch, and said in a controlled, nonemotional voice, "I am really angry. I am very upset. I would like to choke their necks. I am going to write them a letter and tell them what I think of them." He carried on like this for about five minutes. At the conclusion of his gentle tirade he took a deep breath, looked at me with a twinkle in his eye, and said, "I feel much better now."

If we are to enjoy the healing that God wants to give us, it's essential for us to acknowledge our emotions and to deal with them as important aspects of who we are. Failure to do so will inevitably hinder our growth and maturity as sons and daughters of the Living God. A friend of mine, Joseph, has discovered this to be true.

Joseph grew up with a strong, domineering mother and an extremely busy father. There were key times in Joseph's development as a teenager when he needed his parents to make an emotional connection with him, to help him identify what he was feeling and to support him as he was working through those feelings. He was going through some fairly normal childhood experiences—in sports, boy/girl relations, and so on—but his mom and dad never connected with him. As a result, Joseph has grown up a one-dimensional guy. There are many things he simply can't identify with; the joys or pains or hurts of other people just don't resonate with him. He said to me on one occasion, "I can't identify with people when they're suffering. In fact, it frightens me. I want to avoid them because I don't know what to do. It's really intimidating to me."

Do you see how serious it can be to try and ignore or stuff our emotions? Doing so keeps us from functioning in a healthy and normal manner. God intends for us to experience emotion, to be able to name the emotion, and to respond to that emotion appropriately. This is part of who we are as human beings. If a person doesn't deal with emotions in a healthy way, the very pain he tries to avoid ends up controlling him!

Enjoy Your Healing

Emotions are like the red light on the dashboard of a car. They are not the *source* of a problem, they are just an *indicator* that a problem exists. Neither do emotions *create* a blessing; they are simply God's way of letting us *enjoy* a blessing.

Can you imagine what it would be like to be a computer or a robot—never knowing elation or sorrow, confidence or fear, love or anger? It's almost impossible for us to conceive of an emotionless being, although there have been some notable attempts to do so. Television's *Star Trek* gave us at least two main characters who lived (or tried to live) without emotion. On the original show, Mr. Spock—half Vulcan, half human—claimed to live by logic alone without any of the encumbrances of emotion. And yet on several occasions—much to his dismay—his logic gave way to outbursts, however short, of genuine emotion. (After all, he was only half human!)

Several years later, *Star Trek: The Next Generation* gave us Lieutenant Commander Data, an android created without an "emotion chip." Yet what was most intriguing about this character—in contrast to Mr. Spock—was that he was constantly *in pursuit* of emotion! He realized he could never be fully human without the ability to feel.

Without emotions, life would be unremittingly boring. Flat. Dull. Uninteresting. It would be like watching an orchestra without being able to hear the elegant music being played. Like chewing a gourmet meal without the ability to taste its delicacies. Like having friendship without affection, a house without heat, or a parade without floats, bands, horses, fire trucks, and clowns.

And who would want that?

Emotions are like the volume control on a good stereo set. With music you really enjoy, you can turn up the dial and clearly hear both the bass and the treble. Listen sometime to great music on a powerful sound system—one with a bazillion amps of power and Dolby digital stereo and surround sound—and you'll soon be *feeling* the depth, passion, intensity, and multiple dimensions of the music.

So it is with emotions. On the one hand they allow us to fully enjoy and experience the best of life, while on the other hand they enable us to fully bear the weight of the more difficult sides of life. They add color to the canvas of life, taste to the palate of experience.

When a person does what is right, we revel in the deep feeling of satisfaction that breaks over us. There's a deep sense of gratitude for a husband who loves his wife, delight for a parent who cares for a little child properly, sorrow for a friend who has lost a loved one. All of these are emotions given by our loving Creator to allow us to experience life more completely.

What Are Emotions For?

Yet as good as emotions are, God did not create us to live *by* emotions; He did not intend for our actions to be determined by what we feel. Rather, He intended for emotions to be an extra benefit to life—to give life a dimension of feeling.

One of the greatest benefits God intended for us by endowing us with emotions—in addition to enhancing our humanity—is that they reinforce righteousness. It's similar to a trailer following a car: The car is to lead, the trailer is to follow. What a mess we would have on our highways if the trailer led the car! God intends for us to live by truth and right choices; emotions then come along and reinforce this. Emotions are the caboose attached to the train engine. They are meant as a support, an encouragement in life, but not to determine where we go or how we live.

This implies, of course, that if we live to gratify our emotions, then life inevitably becomes twisted. It's as if we're trying to follow a map that's been misprinted. We think we're going west when we're really going east, and we wind up in Siberia rather than Los Angeles—which could be a major problem if you arrive in twenty-below weather and six feet of snow while dressed in Bermuda shorts and beach sandals. A misprinted map will likely lead you in a wrong—and perhaps disastrous—direction. You'll inevitably come to dead ends, unfinished roadways, and will be forced to deal with unfulfilled expectations and the accompanying frustration and even heartache (not to mention frostbite).

Emotions are wonderful, but they are not paramount. They are delightful companions, but not leaders of the pack. The truth is, emotions in themselves can never finally or fully satisfy. They can gratify only truth; they cannot gratify selfishness. Yet many of us forget this in a headlong rush to live by our emotions.

For example, Ernest Hemingway once said, "Good is what you feel good after; bad is what you feel bad after." He was saying that truth is determined by your feelings. If it *feels* good after you do something, then it *was* good. If it *feels* like the right thing to have done, then it *was* the right thing to do. Of course, there are serious drawbacks to such a perspective. Hemingway himself could tell you so if he were available for comment. Unfortunately, he's not. On July 2, 1961, while wallowing in an anxiety-ridden and depressed state, he put a shotgun to his head and pulled the trigger.

As I said, living by emotions does have its downside. All of us recognize there is a deceptive nature to emotions; we know they can betray us. Our conscience can be seared, allowing us to do evil and harmful things and yet feel good about what we have done—like the bank robber who, in the camaraderie of a band of thieves, feels elated that he has gotten away with his crime. The criminals reinforce one another's joy when they celebrate over what they accomplished. But in reality, they have stolen from the poor and endangered the lives of innocent men and women. Their emotions are not an accurate barometer of the truth.

We must be careful because our emotions can deceive us. It is possible, for example, to believe that a person has rejected us or is criticizing us or has something against us when, in fact, the person *may not feel or think anything close to what we believe they do.*

A friend of mine once told me about a female co-worker who spent her first year and a half with their company falsely believing that he hated her (they now are good friends). It happened like this: My friend has a tendency to concentrate so fully on a project that he fails to disengage mentally from that project even when interrupted. Often when the woman entered my friend's office to chat, he was slow to greet her and seldom turned to face her right away. She took this as rejection and speedily retreated to her own cubicle, imagining that the "cold reception" meant her new colleague hated her. Therefore every time she interacted with him she responded anxiously and quickly withdrew to her office. Meanwhile, my friend was oblivious both to his inhospitality and to the effect it was having on his new coworker. He assumed she was just a wee bit too tightly wound-up!

The truth was, both of them were acting on perceptions that had nothing to do with the truth. My friend did *not* hate his new coworker and she did *not* suffer from a bad case of nerves. Yet because they failed to work through the situation to get to the real problem, they missed out on a year and a half of a delightful friendship.

Is It Godly to Show Emotion?

Some people think God frowns on us when we talk honestly about our emotions. These people live with a fear that it's unspiritual to say things like, "I am unhappy," "I am sad," "I am angry," "I am fearful," "I am frightened," "I am discouraged," or "I am depressed." Their definition of spirituality will not allow them to acknowledge how they are feeling, for fear that God will reject them or that others will misunderstand them.

But is that true? Will God be upset if we tell Him the truth about how we feel?

As no doubt you would expect, I don't think that's true at all. God is not angry with us when we admit our emotions; in fact, He insists that is exactly what we are to do. Let me explain how I know that.

First, it's important to remember that Jesus told us that the truth sets us free (John 8:32). We can't receive the truth, however, if we are not truthful about how we feel. Denying how we feel makes it almost impossible for us to admit we have a need. That's what Jesus was getting at when He told the Pharisees, "It is not the healthy who need a doctor, but the sick. I have not come to call the righteous, but sinners" (Mark 2:17). The Master was saying that the first step toward spiritual health is admitting that we are desperately sick.

Being truthful about how we feel lets us recognize how we are reacting to other people, events, or circumstances. Our reactions may well be wrong, but being truthful about our feelings allows us to identify that they *are* wrong. Then we can take the next step and fix the problem.

Second, we find many people in the Bible who are surprisingly honest about their emotions—far more honest than we generally dare to be. The Scripture lifts up as great heroes men and women who often expressed their anger, fear, disappointment, or jealousy. Let me cite just a few examples.

+ *David,* whom the Bible calls "a man after [God's] own heart" (1 Samuel 13:14) and "the apple of [God's] eye" (Psalm 17:8), felt free to pour out his discouragement and disappointment to God: "How long, O LORD? Will you forget me forever? How long will you hide your face from me?" (Psalm 13:1). When was the last time you talked to God like that?

+ *Jonah,* the runaway prophet, was displeased and angry that God did not wipe out Nineveh and admitted his feelings to the Lord: "I am angry enough to die," he told Him (Jonah 4:1,9).

+ *Paul,* the great apostle, was unashamed to write to his Roman friends about his feelings for the spiritual condition of his Jewish countrymen: "I have great sorrow and unceasing anguish in my heart.... for the sake of my brothers" (Romans 9:2-3).

+ *Jacob,* one of the patriarchs, more than once did not hesitate to admit his fear: "I was afraid...I am afraid" (Genesis 31:31; 32:11; *see also* 32:7).

Throughout the Bible we find men and women relating to God with brutal honesty. The Scriptures unashamedly record how men and women responded emotionally to the Lord Jesus and to God. We recall how disappointed Mary and Martha were with Jesus; how Moses flushed with anger; how Rachel burned with jealousy; how Jeremiah agonized with fear and tears; how Solomon admitted his insecurity. The list could go on and on. My point is that not only are emotions themselves good, but so is *admitting* the emotion we are feeling—whether that emotion is an expression of godliness or not.

God is not displeased with us when we admit the emotions we feel. While it may be that He won't want us to remain in the emotional state we confess, you can rest assured He never grows angry with us for expressing the emotion we feel in our heart.

How could He? After all, He's an emotional God Himself!

SETTING OUR FEELINGS FREE

God's Emotions

Have you ever thought about the emotional life of God? Some of us are so used to thinking about God as the omnipotent, omniscient, immutable, holy, and righteous Lord of the universe that we forget He has *feelings*. Real feelings. Deep feelings. Feelings that leave no doubt about His emotional nature.

Just consider a handful of the emotions Scripture attributes to God:

- *Love* (Exodus 20:6; 1 John 3:1; 4:8)

- *Anger, wrath* (Numbers 11:10; Revelation 19:15)

- *Happiness* (Isaiah 42:1; Matthew 25:21,23)

- *Grief* (Genesis 6:6; Ephesians 4:30)

- *Joy* (Psalm 104:31; John 15:11; 17:13)

- *Jealousy* (Exodus 20:5; 1 Corinthians 10:22)

- *Satisfaction* (Isaiah 53:11; Matthew 3:17)

- *Disgust* (Leviticus 18:22; Luke 16:15)

- *Compassion* (Hosea 11:8; 2 Corinthians 1:3)

- *Hatred* (Amos 5:21; Revelation 2:6)

It doesn't take a Bible scholar to see that the God of the Scriptures is no pale, anemic, dreary deity who dispassionately fiddles with the universe throughout an apathetic and indifferent eternity. The Bible pictures a God who is bursting with emotion. It presents a God longing for the day when He can belt out an unrestrained song of pure delight in His redeemed people

64

(Zephaniah 3:17). It describes a God whose anger can level mountains and raise up valleys, whose love can bring heaven to earth, and whose joy can cause the rivers and trees and rocks to shout with resounding praise.

No, God has never been bashful about showing His emotions and naming them for what they are. He has refused to remain aloof from us and distant from us. He has entered into our world. He has taken it upon Himself to become a man like us, and the Bible insists that He has and expresses emotions just like us.

We see the same thing in the life of Jesus. Don't believe some film versions of the life of Christ which present Him as a kind of antiseptic holy man floating a foot off the ground, traveling untouched and unfeeling through our hurting world. The real Jesus could be indignant (Mark 10:14), angry (Mark 3:5), compassionate (Luke 15:20), joyful (John 15:11), deeply sorrowful (Matthew 26:38), astonished (Matthew 8:10), aggravated (Matthew 17:17), and hurt (John 6:67). In the garden just before He was arrested, He prayed with intense feeling as He pled with His Father to spare Him the agony of the cross.

So you see, Jesus was unflinchingly honest with His own feelings and with how He related to His friends. He expects no less from us.

Be Honest with Your Emotions

God wants us to express our emotions and be honest with Him about what is happening in our life. It's the only way we can receive the appropriate grace to grow. Stuffing our emotions and refusing to be honest about them produces in us a sense of hopelessness.

I've often asked the question, "Why do some people grow more quickly than others?" I've seen young Christians who come out of difficult pasts grow quickly, while others with similar backgrounds grow hardly at all. Why? What makes the difference?

I'm convinced that one big reason is honesty. Some people grow quickly because they are unafraid to be honest about what they feel and to name their needs. They come to God with such gratefulness, such vulnerability, such openness. On the other hand, those who seem to take ages to grow build walls around themselves, refuse to disclose their emotions, and will not admit their needs. They don't grow because they cannot receive God's grace, for the only way to receive grace is to admit that you need it!

Psalm 51:6 tells us that God wants us to be honest with Him at the deepest levels. "Surely you desire truth in the inner parts; you teach me wisdom in the inmost place," David writes. David was saying that God wanted him to live truthfully at the very depth of his being, at the very core. He was to pour out all that was in his heart and allow God to deal with his true condition.

This doesn't imply that all of our emotions will be pure or pleasant! They certainly won't be. Shortly before Jonah confessed he was angry that God had spared Nineveh, the Lord asked the prophet, "Have you any right to be angry?" (Jonah 4:4). The definite implication is that Jonah had *no* right to be angry. Still, he was angry; and to deny it would have short-circuited God's work in his life.

If we begin by admitting what emotion is in our heart—right or wrong—then and only then can we move forward to live the way God wants us to live. Suppose somebody offends me and I become angry with him. I can't forgive him until I am honest and say, "I am offended." But when I am honest about that, then I can take the next step and move to forgive him in earnest.

Being honest about our feelings also allows us to face temptations, resist them, and overcome them. If we don't acknowledge the temptation for what it is, it can grow in our life and become a powerful stumbling block. By denying that we are tempted, we make it much easier to succumb to the temptation. On the other hand, when we face the temptation and admit, "I'm tempted to lie, steal, lust, or gossip," and by being honest about why the temptation is attractive, we can arm ourselves against caving in.

We can't suppress such negative emotions. We must be honest with them, admit them, and deal with them in a godly way. Perhaps this means we need to go to someone and say, "I'm struggling with feeling rejected by you. Can we talk about this? Did you intend to say what I thought I heard you say? I found it hurtful."

Swearing Men, Crying Women

We live in a culture that allows women to cry and not swear, and men to swear but not cry. In other words, men can show passion and intensity about their negative feelings, but rarely are they permitted to weep over those emotions. On the other hand, women are allowed to cry often but are not encouraged to express intense, strong, or extreme negative emotions.

The moral of this little observation is not that men and women should go around both swearing and crying, but that both men and women should be honest about feelings of anger and hurt. We should not allow our culture to dictate to us how we respond to our feelings. We should be godly about how we deal with them, but godly does not mean we contain those emotions. Godly means we honestly acknowledge them and then deal with them in a way that honors God.

Being honest like this allows us to keep our relationships free of barriers or hindrances. It does no good to attack an emotion if we don't understand it. It's like swinging a hammer at the red light on the dashboard; that won't solve our problem. The only thing that will do is ensure that we'll soon see a tow truck pulling our disabled car.

We must be honest about our emotions, good and bad. That doesn't mean we use a megaphone to broadcast a running description of our feelings to everyone within earshot! But it does mean we need to take seriously what our emotion is and trace it down to its source.

Identifying Our Emotions

We have been given, as God's creation, a delightful capacity for emotions. Sadly, however, not all of us are adept at identifying the emotions we feel.

SETTING OUR FEELINGS FREE

I've known many people who carried deep emotional scars resulting from manipulation, alcoholism in their home, drug abuse among family members, workaholic or absent parents, excessive anger, or verbal or physical abuse. Painful emotional scars like these make it difficult for them to know what to do with their emotions, especially if they can't express them or identify what those emotions are and put a label on them.

It's crucial that we be able to identify our emotions—to name them, to connect an appropriate term with the feeling in our heart. So with that in mind, I'd like you to take time out now for a little "test." This is the "Name That Feeling" test.

How would each of the following scenarios make you feel if they happened to you?

+ You wake up face-down on the pavement.

+ You put your bra on backwards...and it fits better.

+ You call suicide prevention and they put you on hold.

+ You see a "60 Minutes" news team waiting for you in your office.

+ Your birthday cake collapses from the weight of the candles.

+ You turn on the news and they're showing emergency routes that lead out of the city.

+ Your twin sister forgets your birthday.

✦ Your car alarm goes off by accident and remains stuck as you follow a group of Hell's Angels on the freeway.

✦ Your boss tells you not to bother with taking off your coat when you come into the office.

✦ Your wife says, "Good morning, Bill," and your name is George.

Sorry, but I couldn't resist! This short quiz wasn't terribly hard, was it? I excerpted these scenarios from an article titled, "Signs That It's Going to Be a Rotten Day." I hope you enjoyed these as much as I did the first time I read them!

Unfortunately, not all emotions are as easy to identify as these. Some of us were parented in such a way that we are unaccustomed to talking about how we feel. Talking about our feelings makes us uncomfortable because we grew up in a family in which it was never practiced. In fact, it may have been taboo to mention how you felt.

If your parents never talked honestly about how they felt, then it's likely you don't know how to verbalize your emotions. If that describes you, then allow me to give you this one bit of advice: *It's time to learn!*

To begin, I think it might be helpful for us to list some terms that describe common emotions. I go through this routine every once in a while and find it helpful when I can't figure out what I'm feeling. I actually go down the following list and think, *What am I feeling about this?* The list I use has three major categories: sad words; glad words; mad words.

Sad Words

- ✦ Disappointment
- ✦ Hurt
- ✦ Grieved
- ✦ Wounded
- ✦ Discouraged
- ✦ Afraid
- ✦ Ashamed
- ✦ Condemned

Glad Words

- ✦ Happy
- ✦ Excited
- ✦ Enthused
- ✦ Delighted
- ✦ Thrilled
- ✦ Peaceful
- ✦ Thankful
- ✦ Grateful

Mad Words

- ✦ Angry
- ✦ Upset

+ Frustrated

+ Peeved

+ Impatient

+ Bitter

+ Hateful

If you struggle with naming the emotion you feel, you might find it helpful to sit down with a thesaurus and the foregoing lists and write out as many related terms as you can find. A good thesaurus will not only suggest words that are more or less identical in meaning to the one you've looked up, but also will give several related terms that slightly differ in nuance.

When you look up *angry*, for example, you might see the following: "irate, mad, wrathful, provoked, warlike, ireful, enraged, aggravated, annoyed, cross, fuming, furious, hot, incensed, teed-off, upset," along with such synonyms as "blow up, boil, bristle, burn, flare, fume, rage, seethe, hot under the collar, hit the ceiling, see red."

I suggest you spend some time creating an expanded list in all the categories previously mentioned. Look for words that connect with you, that seem to describe feelings you have. Then when you are confused about an emotion you feel and can't seem to identify it, get out your expanded list and look for a term that appears to get close to how you're feeling. Once you've identified and named the emotion, you'll find it much easier to deal with.

Looking Out for Others

It's important for us not only to be able to identify and name our own emotions, but to be sensitive to the emotions and feelings of those around us. God is not pleased when we seek emotional healing for ourselves but bludgeon everyone around us.

Some time ago in the sheep country of New Mexico, some shepherds were worried because they were losing lambs in the late winter and early spring.[1] The ewes would take their lambs out to graze and never noticed that late in the day the temperature would drop and it would start to snow. While the ewes continued to graze, the lambs would lie down on the ground—and before long, would freeze to death.

Eventually, the shepherds realized that the ewes, covered with wool from head to toe, didn't feel the temperature dropping. So they came up with a unique solution. They sheared the wool on top of the ewes' heads. Then when the weather changed, the ewes felt the drop in temperature, headed back to the barn, and the lambs followed—thus saving their lives.

You know, sometimes our own hearts get all warm and woolly. We enjoy our good fortune and are thankful for it. And there's nothing wrong with enjoying the warm, fuzzy feeling we get from our thick, woolly coat. The problem is, we can get to the point where we become insensitive to the pain of others. We no longer feel what others are feeling. They may be dying, but we don't see it.

Maybe the Holy Spirit needs to shear our hearts of some of the wool so we can feel the hurts and pains of those around us. Then we may enter into their lives with God's grace and the good news and the healing power of Christ.

Barriers to Our Healing

There *are* barriers to our healing. But God's willingness to heal is not one of them. He wants to step into the pain in our life, to bear our burden with us, and set us free. When we realize that God has borne the pain of the world on Himself, we have taken a major step toward real healing.

Sadly, the existence of "real healing" also implies there is such a thing as "false healing"—that is, the false solutions for dealing with our pain. So let me say it again: If we don't actively look to God to deal with our pain and what causes it, we will look elsewhere. And those "elsewheres" are the things we do to find meaning or security—things we pursue to heal us but which never can.

Some of these false solutions have to do with emotions. We are responsible for discerning what is true and what is false, and the Bible offers some practical helps for developing such discernment. That's what I would like to talk about in the next chapter.

4

THAT'S NO WAY TO GET HEALED!

*A*n adoring young public thought Kurt Cobaine had it all. As the 27-year-old lead singer for the rock band Nirvana, Cobaine enjoyed wealth, fame, and influence. Married to a beautiful young woman, worshiped by his fans, and lionized by music critics, the rock star was thrust (against his wishes) to the top of the music world. Nirvana's first album sold over nine million copies. Kurt was on top of a mountain; it was all his.

Yet on April 7, 1994, Kurt put a shotgun to his head and pulled the trigger, leaving his wife a widow and his fans shell-shocked. News reports said Cobaine shot himself because of depression and drug abuse and added that he had tried to commit suicide just one month before.

"ABC Nightly News" interviewed one of Cobaine's many fans shortly after the suicide, a young man who couldn't fathom what had happened. "When you reach that level of fame and still are not happy," he said unbelievingly, "something must be wrong."[1]

Something *was* wrong—but it had nothing to do with fame or popularity. A Seattle cab driver who had often chauffeured Cobaine around town described the late musician as a "nice young man. Very quiet. But I guess he had a lot of hurtin'."[2]

Kurt Cobaine—rock star, teen idol, unofficial spokesman for a generation—was a man who vainly tried to find release from his deep pain. In despair, he took his own life.

Sadly, Kurt is not the exception in our society. Though his end was tragic and his attempts at finding answers were extreme, his story is not an unusual one. People in pain are desperately searching for help, but all too often they're finding wrong answers that lead only to more pain.

True and False Healing

A supermarket full of true and false healings are constantly being touted to us today. All of these healings are reported to offer happiness, wholeness, and health. Our problem is that we need to identify which claims are true and which are false.

Suppose you had a favorite tree that was diseased. What would you do? You wouldn't go to somebody who specialized in cutting down trees. Neither would you hire someone whose own yard was full of sick and dying wood. If you wanted to save the tree, you'd call a tree doctor—even though tree doctors often prescribe radical treatments for their patients. They might cut the tree, apply sticky pastes to it, or perform any number of other drastic remedies.

Of course, it would be a lot simpler to call in a witch doctor to dance around your tree. But if your goal was to save your tree, you'd never entertain such a notion.

Yet that brings up a question. If we wouldn't entrust our trees to witch doctors, why do we so often entrust ourselves to modern-day witch doctors?

The sad truth is, we have herds of new age healers who are all too eager to use their magic arts to try to heal the hurts of the human soul—something that only the Creator of the "tree," of the human spirit, is capable of doing.

If we truly want to be healed, we must forget about the human-healers and entrust ourselves to the Great Physician—even if that true healing might require radical treatments.

The Curse of Sin

When are radical treatments necessary? When something is radically wrong. In the case of trees, it might be Dutch Elm disease, beetle infestations, or a fungus. In the case of people, the diagnosis usually boils down to something called *sin*. Though we don't find it pleasant to relate our pain to the concept of sin, the two are so intertwined it is impossible to separate them. In fact, we could say that all pain is caused by sin—either our own or the sins that others commit against us.

All of us are created with God-given capacities for love, relationship, significance, conscience, and creativity. When these capacities and desires become marred and out-of-kilter through the experiences of life and through sin, we *hurt*. God wants to restore these parts of our personality and being to their intended state, but this will never happen if we don't seek true healing from the One who created us.

The very capacities and gifts given to us by God can turn into destructive forces if we don't recognize the potential for evil within every one of us. Sin is not merely a distant concept conjured up by theologians endlessly debating esoteric issues in faraway ivory towers. Perhaps a more concrete way to talk about sin is to consider things like child abuse, rape, racism, anger violence, exploitation, and untold other hurtful acts that help us see how selfish we can be as human beings.

In Romans 6:23, when Paul says that "the wages of sin is *death*," he has in mind spiritual death. But throughout his letter it is clear he understands that this death spreads its deadly fingers into every corner of our experience, not just the eternal state. Three chapters earlier, for example, he gives us an ugly list of just a few particular sins and their consequences: lying, vicious, cursing tongues; feet quick to shed blood; ruin and misery as a way of life; and failure to know peace (Romans 3:10-17).

We will have more to say about sin later, but for now I think it's important that we be honest and admit we're all infected *with* it and deeply affected *by* it. It's critical that we label sin for what it is and not try to camouflage it under the bogus labels of "mistakes," "errors," or "regrettable incidents." That applies to both our own sin and the sins of others committed against us. There are such things as mistakes and errors and regrettable incidents, but when the real culprit is sin, we must call it what it is. Unless we do this, we can never take responsibility for our sins, nor will we be able to forgive others for the sins they have committed against us.

Some counselors and therapists go to the extreme of trying to inflate a person's self-esteem and ego so he will simply feel better about life, but that is treating the symptom alone without getting to the cause of the pain. Of course, having a positive mental attitude *does* have its place—perhaps it will make you an easier person to work with or a better spouse. But it will not solve the problem that has caused the pain.

On the other extreme we find some people who practice what might be called worm psychology—loathe yourself, do-good wretched worm, get it together, get over it. That approach does nothing more than slap emotional Band-Aids on serious pain problems.

It's been my observation that the false healing approaches and panaceas that are offered to us swing like a pendulum between these two extremes. But the fact is, hurts and wounds are not healed by feel-good remedies, get-over-it exhortations, or quick fixes that offer a lot but fail to deliver as advertised. Unfortunately, there are a lot of superficial remedies on the market today—even in Christian circles.

Wounds and pains will never go away by denying they exist, and they will never get healed with superficial love. So what is the answer? How do we get healed? And where do we find the true solutions?

False Solutions to Healing

Before we start looking in depth at God's prescription for healing our hurts, it might be helpful to consider some of the false solutions that are practiced today. Some of these solutions just come naturally to us, and others are on the market because unscrupulous individuals have learned there is money to be made by preying on the pain of a vulnerable public.

1. *Blame shifting*

When the Eagles (a popular rock band of the seventies) released a live album from a reunion tour, they included a new song called, "Get Over It." One of the group's leaders, Don Henley, described it as their contribution to "political incorrectness." The song took head-on the victim mentality and encouraged people to take responsibility for their own actions. You can't continue to blame mommy and daddy for every bad thing you've ever done, the Eagles admonished us.

Unfortunately, many of us continue to try.

A well-known pastor in the Los Angeles area stunned his congregation a few years ago when he unexpectedly delivered a resignation letter to his church. The pastor wrote, "With my recent facing of issues dating from childhood, years of denial and faulty coping techniques, it is becoming clear I have inappropriately tried in my own strength to work through my problems.... Along the way I have stepped over the line of acceptable behavior with some members of the congregation...."[3]

In the pastor's mind, his moral failure wasn't the problem; the problem was that "some members of the congregation" believed that getting involved with someone other than your wife was "stepping over the line of acceptable behavior." Perhaps it would have been better for the pastor to say, "I sinned. I betrayed the trust of my wife. The Bible calls it sin, and I did it." Yet he didn't do that.

The blame-shifting technique obviously works well when it comes to the devil. Since he's never around physically to defend himself, he's an easy target to blame for all the wrong things we do.

I was traveling down the freeway with a friend some years ago. He was driving way over the speed limit and I reminded him of the fact. He looked at me and said, quite seriously, "I can't help it. Something comes over me. I just have to drive fast."

"Sort of like a demon of speed, you mean?" I replied.

"Yes, that's it. I can't control it."

At just that moment, a flashing red light appeared in the rearview mirror. It amazed me how quickly my friend could bring his demon under control when that red light flashed.

I've also noticed that bank robbers who are "demon possessed" don't usually rob banks in front of armed policemen. Children who "can't help" stealing cookies from the cookie jar never do it in front of parents. And students don't cheat on tests in front of the watching eyes of professors or teachers who happen to be standing over their desks.

I have said (more or less jokingly) to a couple of men who were dating my daughter, "Lay a hand on my girl, and I'll break your legs." I wanted these young

men to have enough fear of God (or of Floyd, which-
ever they needed in greater amounts) to encourage them
to treat Misha with respect.

In our day, parents are also the targets of a lot of
blame shifting. After listening to some of today's radio
and TV talk shows, you'd get the impression that parents are the root of all evil. Kids never do anything
wrong; their actions are always the parent's fault—
even if the kid is 75 years old and the parents are in
their late nineties.

I once saw a cartoon that depicted a huge audito-
rium rented for a convention of The Society of Children Raised by Normal Parents. Four people were in
attendance.

Are parents to be blamed for everything? Obviously not. I think it's fair to talk about parental envi-
ronments that produce strong temptations, but we can
never claim that parents *cause* our problems. David Powlison, a Westminster Seminary professor, was asked
about this very question.[4] "Research reveals that children who grow up in one-parent families are more
likely to have social, educational, and psychological
problems," the interviewer said. "Doesn't this demon-
strate a need for love, and that if one doesn't receive
that love from other human beings—"

"—one is destined for a life of crime and misery,"
Powlison interjected.

"Well, not *destined,* but ..." stammered the interviewer.

"See, that's where the crux comes," Powlison continued, "because if they're not destined, then it's not

need in the absolute sense. I think it would be more accurate to say that parents who don't love their children, who abuse them or are manipulative, throw all sorts of stumbling blocks in a child's path. They tempt a child severely, yet you will always have the exceptions: those who had the exact same upbringing but turn out differently.

"Instead of *needs,* I would argue, the conditions of our environment produce certain typical *temptations.* So it's no surprise that those who are abused struggle with rage and mistrust, for instance.

"What radicalized me was thinking about what happens when parents are very good—they're loving, they're caring, they cherish their children. Did the children grow up sin-free? Of course not. Being affirmed brings a whole different set of temptations."

It's good to be honest and say, "Yeah. My parents abused me, or manipulated me." That's important. If you were ripped off by your parents because they weren't there for you, be honest and admit it. But don't make them responsible for all your choices. The Bible says, "The soul who sins is the one who will die" (Ezekiel 18:4) and, "In those days people will no longer say, 'The fathers have eaten sour grapes, and the children's teeth are set on edge.' Instead, everyone will die for his own sin; whoever eats sour grapes—his own teeth will be set on edge" (Jeremiah 31:29-30).

I know of at least one university student who needs to hear the truth of those verses. The student's professor had given his class an opportunity to evaluate the course. One person wrote on his evaluation, "I like the course, but I feel very strongly that the professor puts too much responsibility on the students for learning."

Talk about sour grapes!

Because our sense of personal value is so strongly tied to how we think other people see us, we are often quick to blame others in order to defend our own sense of self-worth. We are amazingly adept as human beings at evaluating others based on our perception of personal success or failure. We can end up blaming people out of fear of being rejected or unfairly punished by them. Fear of failure is a powerful motivator in behavior and attitudes.

This is especially true in relation to people who are close to us. Because we view those closest to us as a reflection on ourselves, we may try to control their behavior to protect ourselves. Those who cause us to "look bad" are "wrong." *They should be punished,* we think to ourselves. Blaming them is a natural means of self-protection.

Being self-protective keeps us from seeing our own faults and weaknesses. We are quick to see the weaknesses of others, but we tend to be blind to our own faults and flesh patterns. It is easy to point out where others are wrong—blame shifting—but difficult to see ourselves as we really are.

2. *Behavior adjustment*

In case you hadn't noticed, a vast self-improvement movement is sweeping the United States. A growing chorus of voices is saying, "Adjust your personality, adapt your behavior, think positively, feel good, and discover wholeness."

All you have to do to see the extent of this movement is spend a few minutes in a bookstore and note all the self-help books that line the shelves. Here are just a few titles I noticed during a recent five-minute browsing session:

+ *52 Ways to Build Your Self-Esteem and Confidence*
+ *Healing Life's Hidden Addictions*
+ *The Self-Talk Solution*
+ *How to Live Between Office Visits*
+ *Ten Days to Self-Esteem*
+ *Believe and Achieve*
+ *Pulling Your Own Strings*
+ *Direct Your Subconscious*

And for the mother of all self-help books, there was . . .

+ *Life's Big Instruction Book* (a whopping 881 pages long!)

But behavior modification can never be a final answer. How could it? It ignores or coddles a person's inner pain and concentrates solely on outer action. At best, it's a Band-Aid.

Nevertheless, legion are the gurus who actively promote some version or another of behavior modification—even in Christian settings. I recently heard one

Christian leader tell a group of pastors, "If you are hurting, the key to healing yourself is taking on responsibility."

I disagree. Who would think of telling a child with a broken arm to deal with his pain by getting a shovel and digging ditches? Additional activity does nothing to deal with the pain itself. It might mask the hurt for awhile, but in the end the suffering will be all the worse.

3. *Pretend it's not there*

We call this denial; ignore the problem and it will go away. A currently popular religious version of this view maintains that faith is acting as if you don't have a problem. To admit you have a problem is to admit you don't have faith. Therefore, if you get a cold, you don't admit such a thing (that would show lack of faith); instead, you must confess to other people that what *looks* like a cold and *sounds* like a cold and produces *fluids* remarkably similar to those associated with a cold is instead merely the devil putting the symptoms of a cold on you.

I have my doubts, though.

We can't deny the truth by using cherished religious words or phrases, whether they're from the faith movement inside the church or from the positive-thinking movement outside the church. True biblical faith looks a problem in the eye and says, "That's the problem. I sinned; I did it. God sees it, I see it, and it's real. *But I believe God is greater than the problem* and that together with Him, I can face it." That's true biblical faith.

4. *Happy hand-holding*

Superficial Christian love is running amok in some circles. Instead of dealing courageously and honestly with the real root of our problems, we instead organize happy hand-holding sessions. Happy hand-holding by-passes the hard edges of truth and instead tries to find healing in a fuzzy, shapeless kind of sentimentality that tries to pass itself off as Christian love. In a genuine effort to be compassionate, happy hand-holders instead imprison a person in a jail of pillows.

I was at a meeting recently where a man stood publicly to acknowledge that he had hurt someone. This man, a leader of stature in the church, asked for prayer. Some people stood and were ready to pray for him on the spot. But before we could do so, another man stood and protested the need for prayer. He said, "We'll get over it!" It was an entirely inappropriate response to the depth of pain the first man felt over his hurtful actions. Happy hand-holding—or in this case, happy back-slapping—does nothing to heal our deep emotional hurts or the hurts we've given to other people as a result of our actions.

Sin is horrific and it has horrific consequences. Whether it is our sin or someone else's, sin is destructive. If a person is to repent and grieve over his sin, we should be sensitive not to rush him through it. A lifelong pattern of sin may require more than five minutes of repentance.

One of my friends was told by a Christian leader that he should take the process of repentance slowly. He did just that. He spent some time asking God to give him a truly repentant and broken heart. As a result, this friend has witnessed a great change in his life.

I'm not encouraging self-effort when I talk about taking time to repent. What I am advocating is that we allow God to truly break our heart over sin. If we are truly in agony about a sin we committed, it's appropriate for us to call that sin what it is and face the emotional weight of what we did—especially if it caused hurt in the lives of other people. Only then can we move on to the next step of forgiveness.

I believe there are times when we or other people have real depths of feeling, of shame and guilt, and we should not rush the process of repentance in such times. Nor should we take a slap-happy approach to the depths of despair or hurt that we or other people feel.

5. High-voltage emotional fixes

Some people seek their healing through what I call high-voltage emotional experiences. Unfortunately, people who are attracted to this source of hoped-for healing often develop an addiction to the emotional highs they get at conferences, church concerts, revival meetings, deliverance sessions, and therapist appointments.

We *should* thank God for the out-of-the-ordinary emotional experiences that we get in life, but we should not seek them as normative. The Bible instructs us to appropriate the power and grace of the indwelling Christ to help us deal with our problems. We are not to run to a faraway city or special conference to look for some high octane solution.

And if we're struggling with knowing how to appropriate God's power, it's appropriate to ask for help. I'm not against asking qualified Christian counselors or mature brothers or sisters in Christ for assistance in overcoming painful experiences in our life. Rather, I'm warning against getting into the habit of flying from one emotional high to another.

To be frank, that's one reason I'm somewhat skeptical about some of the revival movements of our day. I hear about hundreds of sincere believers who travel thousands of miles to flock to receive a high-voltage renewal blessing. But that isn't the answer. If you are a believer in Jesus Christ, all the power that raised Jesus from the dead is in you. You don't need to touch someone's garment (other than Jesus', that is) or make a pilgrimage to a distant city to take advantage of that power. When we need help, wouldn't it be better to turn to the Creator of the Universe who dwells within us?

6. Emotional streaking

It's almost avant-garde in our generation to bare all and describe in detail every shameful particular of our past. We're certainly encouraged to do so by the example of the talk shows, from the weird to the wonderful—Donahue, Geraldo, Sally Jesse Rafael, and all the late-night clones. They keep coming up with something new and sensational to maintain their ratings.

Sadly, a similar trend is plaguing the church today. We see a kind of superficial honesty that's not complete; it's "emotional streaking." The confessors rarely take responsibility for what causes their pain and hurt.

While it is important to take our emotions seriously and face them honestly, it's also crucial to realize that some things are simply better left unsaid. God does not expect us to tell everybody everything. In fact, Scripture insists that some things should remain unspoken (*see* Ephesians 5:12). This would apply equally to group therapy and counseling sessions in which people are encouraged to speak openly of the shameful details of their sexual sins. I am convinced we don't need to tell all to everybody or feel obligated to reveal to other people every evil thing we've ever done.

Let me be very honest here—perhaps uncomfortably honest. We shouldn't be talking openly about the details of our sex life, masturbation, and all the other lurid topics that fill up books, testimonies, and confessions today. I don't want to hear such things in public confessions or testimonies, and I know a lot of other people don't either. In fact, people sometimes come to me and say, "I felt grieved when I read this book" or, "When I heard that person's testimony, I felt unclean." We must be careful about adopting a cultural value that is not based on a biblical principle.

At the same time, it is very helpful to break the power of "secret sin" by confessing it to a godly person (not someone who has the same weakness you do!). Such a person can confirm that we have been open and honest and that God has provided for our forgiveness in Christ. And acting in this way complies with the directives of Matthew 18:15-20 and James 5:16.

7. *Quick fixes*

Who we are is the result of a complex combination of emotions, choices, circumstances, and spiritual battles. Thus it isn't realistic to say that a person can get healed by dealing with that complexity in simple ways. The only truly simple solution I know of is the cross of Jesus Christ, but even then we must apply the cross to those flesh patterns we have held onto in our lives.

During a recent trip to Palm Springs, California, I noticed an intriguing article in the local paper. It was headlined, "Is society searching for quick-fix psychotherapy?"[5] Under the subhead "Fast Freud," the story describes a culture in which people are trying anything that promises a quick fix for their problems. "Brief therapy is a sizzling topic here at the annual conference of the American Association for Marriage and Family Therapy," said the article. "Increasingly, the profession is talking about a form of therapy that lasts perhaps fewer than 10 sessions—with numbers geared to company insurance plans—to treat increasingly difficult problems. The focus in brief therapy is treating symptoms, not changing personalities."

One therapist even advertised a video which he claimed could cure a phobia in five minutes. Some attendees at the conference expressed concern about the trend toward brief therapy, but it certainly fits the American way. People want something quick that will take care of deep problems—even if the solution deals only with the symptoms.

The truth is, quick fixes don't heal us. Spiritual formulas, 1-2-3 steps, and attending spiritual conferences where people divulge spiritual "secrets" might help us to a certain degree, but these fixes can't deal permanently with deeply entrenched problems. The Lord warned about such fixes in Jeremiah 6:14 when He said, "They dress the wound of my people as though it were not serious. 'Peace, peace,' they say, when there is no peace."

A girl once admitted to me that she struggled with impatience. She told me she had prayed about that and felt the Lord had shown her that I was to pray for her to receive the gift of patience. I told her I would be delighted to pray for her, but I also promised she would not like my prayer. She looked at me with great puzzlement and asked, "Well, why?"

"The Bible says that tribulation worketh patience," I replied, "so I'm going to pray that you will have lots of tribulation in your life."

"But I don't *want* tribulation; I want patience!" she declared.

I never did pray for her.

8. *Performance*

Another way we try to find healing is by performance that pleases others. When we perform, we depend on other people to tell us who we are and that we're okay. We can do this to such an extent that *we end up losing the ability to distinguish between who we really are and what we do to please others.*

Behavior is never senseless or meaningless. It's a reflection of our belief about who we are. But if our value and identity is based on the approval of others, we will always be deeply insecure. We must remember that people change. They get angry with us. They move away. And many are just as uncertain about who they are as we are ourselves! Our society abounds with people chasing after each other for approval—yet never finding it. Why don't they? Because it's the tail chasing the animal. You'll never find healing that way.

When we perform to please other people or God, we are adjusting our actions or attitudes to feel good about ourselves. Performance is based on the lie that the approval of others or God (what we call success) will bring happiness or fulfillment.

Robert McGee says, "Consciously or unconsciously, all of us have experienced this feeling that we must meet certain arbitrary standards to attain self-worth. Failing to do so threatens our security and significance. Such a threat, real or perceived, results in a fear of failure at that point, we are accepting the false belief: I must meet certain standards in order to feel good about myself."[6]

The drive to achieve this illusive happiness is determined, to a certain degree, by our personalities and spiritual gifts—but not entirely. Even great achievers (we call them visionaries) can learn to find their acceptance from God's love and not the approval of people.

High achievers are driven to overcome obstacles and take on difficult challenges to feel they are doing something important or worthwhile in life. Some achievers are driven to gain their sense of self-worth by meeting the needs of others and spending time with them in counseling or caring. Still others feel that success comes from organizing their lives or the lives of those around them. Unfortunately, much of what is done in God's name is "dead works." Performing in God's army does not produce good fruit.

Oh, How We Gain!

Perhaps the first step toward firmly gaining the healing we seek is to recognize that God Himself has borne our pain and provided for our wholeness. He has entered into our pain—and it was not cheap nor was it easy.

Charles Wesley saw this clearly more than two hundred years ago. The first stanza from his great hymn, "And Can It Be, That I Should Gain?" states:

> And can it be that I should gain
> An interest in the Savior's blood?
>
> Died He for me, who caused His pain?
> For me, who Him to death pursued?
>
> Amazing love! how can it be
> That Thou, my God, shouldst die for me?

Yes, God's love *is* amazing, all the more so because Wesley was absolutely right: *We* are the ones who caused *His* pain. Yet through what Jesus accomplished on the cross, we are set free. We are loosed from our chains. They are broken!

But it most emphatically did not come easy, or cheap.

5

GOD'S OWN PAIN

*U*nimaginably brutal. Vicious. Inhuman. Such was
the military occupation of Korea just after the turn
of the century. Atrocities beyond belief were repeatedly
inflicted on a defenseless population, in cold blood, by the
country's invaders. So savage was this reign of terror that
many Koreans to this day carry deep, painful emotional
scars from the ordeal.

Perhaps we can begin to understand why the pain
has lasted so long when we consider one particularly
ghastly incident. When Japan overran Korea in 1910,
one of the first actions the military took was to board
up the churches and deport most of the foreign mission-
aries. The conquerors forbade congregations to meet
and jailed many key Christian leaders. As the Rising
Sun expanded its reach farther and farther across the
Pacific, the persecution intensified.

One pastor repeatedly begged his Japanese over-
lords for permission to meet for services. His requests
were consistently turned down, until at last he was told

he could organize a single service. When the news got out, Christians throughout the area could hardly contain their excitement. They began arriving for the service long before dawn, anxious to worship as a community of God once more. When they shut the doors behind them and began to sing exuberant praises to the Lord, their joy overflowed.

So much so, that they didn't hear the commotion outside the building. As the Koreans sang, the Japanese barricaded the doors, doused the building with kerosene, and set it afire. As smoke began to fill the structure, a few believers realized what was happening and ran for the windows. Immediately they were shot to ribbons.

The awful truth instantly dawned on the pastor, who somehow managed to calm his doomed congregation and lead them in one last hymn. Just before the roof collapsed and the building was engulfed in a blazing inferno, the people sang in one voice the famous words:

At the cross, at the cross
　　Where I first saw the light,
And the burden of my heart rolled away,
It was there by faith I received my sight,
　　And now I am happy all the day!

And then in a roar of flame, they were gone.[1]

Those outside who witnessed the massacre could never forget what they had seen and heard. How could they? Some of those present expressed their outrage not only at the Japanese, but also at God. When man's evil becomes barbaric, it's almost a foregone conclusion that someone will ask, "Where is God? If He can do something, why doesn't He? Is He unmoved by this horror? Is it nothing to Him that these people suffer and perish like this? Doesn't He care?"

Although I have never witnessed such a horror as this, I have counseled my share of people in pain who have asked me similar questions: "Can't God see how badly I'm hurting? Why doesn't He do something?"

I think it's critical for wounded people to recognize that not only is our God a God of deep emotion, but He is also a God who has endured far more pain than we could imagine—even if we had a million lifetimes to try doing so. It would be a gargantuan error to think of our Lord as some far-off, disinterested deity untouched and untouchable by human pain. He not only knows when we are hurting and identifies with us in our pain, but He Himself has also been subjected to a kind of pain we will never, ever be able to fully fathom.

Let me tell you right up front that, after you have read this chapter, *you will never again wonder if God can be touched by your emotions.* God knows when you're hurting. He cares deeply about it. And He Himself has been hurt far more than we will ever know.

The Pain of God

It's a remarkable fact that *none* of the systematic theologies I know of talk about God's emotions. They do a good job of describing the existence of God, His decrees, His attributes, and so forth—yet they rarely, if ever, touch even lightly on our Lord's emotions. Much less do they describe His *pain.*

101

And yet God's pain is mentioned frequently in Scripture as a major motivation for what He does. Without trying to be exhaustive, I would yet like to take you on a brief tour of several biblical passages that describe God's pain. You may be surprised by what you are about to discover.

1. *God experiences great pain over sin*

Almost as soon as the curtains part and the biblical drama begins to unfold, Scripture describes how God's heart was broken over the sinfulness of His creation. "The LORD was grieved that he had made man on the earth, and his heart was filled with pain," says Genesis 6:6. The word translated "grieved" comes from the Hebrew *naham,* which, in other places, is rendered "to be sorry" or "to console oneself." The wrenching phrase "his heart was filled with pain" comes from the Hebrew term *asab,* which always means to be distressed, hurt, or pained.

These pregnant terms show what an immense, infinite grief in the heart of God was created by His great disappointment over His fallen creation. So great was this grief that, according to the very next verse, it prompted God to send the great Flood, which wiped out all of mankind except for Noah and his family. This pain was deep, serious, and overpowering. Genesis 6:6 certainly does not describe a God who can't be hurt or touched by deep emotion!

The Hebrew term *naham* turns up repeatedly when the Bible wants to describe God's intense sorrow over His sinning children. "I am *grieved* that I have made

Saul king, because he has turned away from me and has not carried out my instructions," the Lord says to Samuel (1 Samuel 15:11). And just in case we miss the gravity of His remark, it is repeated a few verses later: "And the LORD was *grieved* that he had made Saul king over Israel" (15:35). Sin always grieves God; it always causes Him pain. That is one of the reasons I said we can never hope to grasp how wide and deep and great His pain has been. Every sin ever committed by every person who ever lived—every lie, every cutting remark, every act of lust, thievery, murder, pride, jealousy, envy, drunkenness, or what have you—has deeply grieved God's loving heart. Can you imagine the cumulative effect? I confess I can't.

The prophet Ezekiel used another graphic term to picture God's pain over His wandering people's affections. "I have been *grieved* by their adulterous hearts," the Lord says, "which have turned away from me, and by their eyes, which have lusted after their idols" (Ezekiel 6:9). Here the Hebrew term is *sabar,* which is usually translated, "to break," "break in pieces," "shatter." It would not be too much to say that Ezekiel is describing a God whose loving heart has been broken to pieces because of the unrestrained infidelity of His beloved children.

2. *God's pain over His people's misery*

Sin is not the only thing that causes pain in the heart of God. Consider the time, for example, when the Lord judged the nation Israel after David organized a census. Thousands of Israelites died at the hands of a destroying angel. The disaster was so profound that Scripture says, "When the angel stretched out his hand to destroy Jerusalem, the LORD was *grieved* [*naham*] because of the calamity and said to the angel who was afflicting the people, 'Enough! Withdraw your hand'" (2 Samuel 24:16, *see also* 1 Chronicles 21:15). Although the cause of the plague was David's sin, it was the great suffering of the people that caused the Lord to grieve. Again, hardly a dispassionate, distant God!

The term *asab*, which Genesis 6:6 used to describe God's pain, can be found in other texts as well. Jeremiah, the weeping prophet, announced the Lord's own words to a rebellious nation that was one step away from exile: "If you stay in this land, I will build you up and not tear you down; I will plant you and not uproot you, for I am *grieved* over the disaster I have inflicted on you" (Jeremiah 42:10).

Note once more that although the Lord brought the disaster in response to His people's sin, what especially grieved Him was the effect the disaster had on the people. He hates to see His beloved people suffer. The Lord is never happy to discipline His children. He does not want to do it. But if that is the only way to get His erring sons and daughters back on the right road, He will use even the most severe methods to do so. We can see His compassionate heart especially in Lamentations 3:31-33, where after witnessing the horrors of a city destroyed, Jeremiah assures us that:

> Men are not cast off
> by the Lord forever.

Though he brings grief, he will show
    compassion,
    so great is his unfailing love.
For he does not willingly bring affliction
    or grief to the children of men.

Isaiah brings out this truth in Isaiah 63:9-10a. He writes, "In all their distress he too was distressed, and the angel of his presence saved them. In his love and mercy he redeemed them; he lifted them up and carried them all the days of old. Yet they rebelled and grieved his Holy Spirit."

The word rendered "distress" here is the Hebrew term *sarah,* which can also be translated "troubles." When the prophet tells us that God was "distressed" by the troubles of His people, he uses the term *sar,* which carries the additional thought of "anguish." So Isaiah is saying that when God saw the difficulties of His people—their troubles, distress, hardships—He was hurt by the sight. It pained him; it caused Him anguish. In response, He roused His almighty right hand to deliver them even to the extent of "carrying" them! Yet despite all this, still they did not understand. Still they rebelled, which Isaiah says "grieved" (*asab* again, as in Genesis 6:6) the Lord.

If you still wonder whether our sorrows and hurts move the heart of God, then read what Judges 10:16 says: "Then they got rid of the foreign gods among them and served the LORD. . . . he could bear Israel's misery no longer."

Have you ever had to stand by and watch a loved one labor and struggle under a burden so heavy it threatened to crush him? Perhaps you watched a son or daughter agonize over a complicated math assignment that they just couldn't understand. Or maybe it was a best friend who was forced to grapple day after grueling day with a surly, unreasonable boss. Or perhaps you stood by helplessly as your spouse battled with depression. Oh, how you wanted to reach out and help that person so precious to you! How you longed to do *something* to make that person's situation better. You watched his or her misery until you could bear to watch it no longer. It pained you beyond description.

That's exactly the picture in Judges 10:16. Yes, Israel had sinned. Yes, the people had strayed. Yes, they had prostituted themselves with foreign gods—and misery was the inevitable result. But when at last they turned from their worthless idols and fled back to the Lord, how did He respond? With anger? No! He responded in love. In joy. With pure delight! Why? Because He loved His people and "he could bear Israel's misery no longer."

3. God's pain overcoming judgment

As powerful as all these word pictures are, however, the most remarkable has to be Hosea 11:8. If there is a cry of pain prompted by unrequited love anywhere in the Old Testament, this is it. By the time this passage was written, God had suffered the faithless wanderings of His people for year upon year, decade upon decade. The time was fast approaching when judgment could not be held back. Yet the Lord could not bear to think of the coming disasters, and He cried:

How can I give you up, Ephraim?
How can I hand you over, Israel?
How can I treat you like Admah?
How can I make you like Zeboiim?
My heart is changed within me;
all my compassion is aroused.

J.B. Hindley comments that "here we get a glimpse of the heart of God. . . . His heart *recoils,* His emotions are in turmoil and His *compassion* glows. He cries in anguish 'How can I?' "[2]

God's anguish is prompted by imminent and severe judgment. These are His people, but He knows disaster cannot be averted much longer; the nation's sin demands an accounting. Yet His divine mind goes back to another scene of disaster, similar to what lies ahead, and He recoils. Admah and Zeboiim were two cities of the plain destroyed along with Sodom and Gomorrah. Their awful fate is pictured in Deuteronomy 29:23: "a burning waste of salt and sulfur—nothing planted, nothing sprouting, no vegetation growing on it. . . . the LORD overthrew [them] in fierce anger."

And now the God who "inhabits eternity,"[3] to whom "one day is like a thousand years, and a thousand years are like a day,"[4] in His mind's eye, sees these two images of catastrophe come together as if they were one terrible event—and His heart breaks.

"How can I?" He asks. "How can I?" He pleads. The impending calamities whip up a boiling, churning emotional turmoil within Him and He admits, "My heart is changed within me; all my compassion is aroused." As He muses on these terrible events, He declares that

He will not utterly destroy Israel, though her many sins deserve such judgment. Though He will severely punish the nation, one day He promises to bring His sons and daughters back and return them to His blessing and favor.

Now, let me ask you: Does this sound like a distant God? Like a God who can remain untouched and unmoved by our hurts and pain? Does this sound like a robot God, a God without emotion or passion or feeling?

Or does it sound like a God whose heart is so emotionally bound up with His children that their pain cannot help but cause Him pain?

That's not a tough question to answer, is it?

4. *God's pain over our weakness*

Not only is God hurt by our sin, misery, and future judgment, but even our weakness causes His heart to break. I think we fail to give enough weight to a particular word in a very famous verse. In Romans 8, Paul waxes eloquent about suffering, glory, hope, freedom, and adoption. He wants to direct our attention to the fabulous future awaiting us, while yet equipping us to function "down here." And so in verse 26 he writes:

> In the same way, the Spirit helps us in our weakness. We do not know what we ought to pray for, but the Spirit himself intercedes for us with groans that words cannot express.

Can you guess which word in this verse is frequently overlooked? It's the little word "groans." I suspect we have been so grateful to learn that the Spirit Himself prays for us when we don't know what to pray for that we have passed by this crucial little word with barely a thought. That's understandable, but regrettable.

What are these "groans"? The word in the original Greek text, *stenagmos,* means much the same thing and is used in much the same way as our English word *groan.* It means, "sigh," "groan," "groaning."[5] The word is used in the New Testament only here and in Acts 7:34. In the latter passage, Stephen is recounting highlights from Israel's history and in so doing repeats God's words spoken just before the Exodus: "I have indeed seen the oppression of my people in Egypt. I have heard their *groaning* and have come down to set them free."

You groan when you are in pain. You groan when something is hurting you. A groan is "a low, mournful sound uttered in pain or grief."[6]

And incredibly, that is exactly what the Holy Spirit of God does for you and me when He prays the prayers we can't. He *groans!*

As one old commentary tells us, "When the Christian's prayers are too deep and too intense for words, when they are rather a sigh heaved from the heart than any formal utterance, then we may know that they are prompted by the Spirit Himself. It is He who is praying to God for us."[7]

And how is He praying? With groans too deep for words. God's Holy Spirit considers us in our weakness—in our limitations, in our frailty—and He is moved with such love and compassion for us that the earnest requests He makes on our behalf come out not in phrases or words, but in emotion-packed groans.

The Pain of the Son

Jesus was every bit a flesh-and-blood man during the time He walked this earth two thousand years ago. He ate. He slept. He worked. He got tired. He sweat. He wondered.

And He felt pain. Let's consider just a few Bible passages in which it is clear Jesus felt pain—real, uncomfortable, sometimes searing pain.

+ John 11:33-35,38—"When Jesus saw her weeping, and the Jews who had come along with her also weeping, he was deeply moved in spirit and troubled. 'Where have you laid him?' he asked. 'Come and see, LORD,' they replied. Jesus wept... Jesus, once more deeply moved...."

+ Matthew 23:37-38—"O Jerusalem, Jerusalem, you who kill the prophets and stone those sent to you, how often I have longed to gather your children together, as a hen gathers her chicks under her wings, but you were not willing. Look, your house is left to you desolate."

+ Luke 19:41-42—"As he approached Jerusalem and saw the city, he wept over it and said, 'If you, even you, had only known on this day what would bring you peace—but now it is hidden from your eyes.'"

+ John 12:27—"Now my heart is troubled, and what shall I say? 'Father, save me from this hour'?

No, it was for this very reason I came to this hour."

✦ John 13:21—"After he had said this, Jesus was troubled in spirit and testified, 'I tell you the truth, one of you is going to betray me.'"

✦ Mark 14:33—"He took Peter, James and John along with him, and he began to be deeply distressed and troubled."

✦ Matthew 26:37-38,40—"He took Peter and the two sons of Zebedee along with him, and he began to be sorrowful and troubled. Then he said to them, 'My soul is overwhelmed with sorrow to the point of death. Stay here and keep watch with me. . . .' Then he returned to his disciples and found them sleeping. 'Could you men not keep watch with me for one hour?' he asked Peter."

The writer of Hebrews apparently had these moving scenes in mind when he wrote, "During the days of Jesus' life on earth, he offered up prayers and petitions with loud cries and tears to the one who could save him from death, and he was heard because of his reverent submission. Although he was a son, he learned obedience from what he suffered" (Hebrews 5:7-8). Later, as the writer began to wind down his book, his mind traveled back once more to these events. That is why he encouraged us to "fix our eyes on Jesus, the author and perfecter of our faith, who for the joy set before him endured the cross, scorning its shame, and sat down at the right hand of the throne of God. Consider him who endured such opposition from sinful men, so that you will not grow weary and lose heart" (Hebrews 12:2-3).

Yes, Jesus knew searing pain—both physical and emotional. But we have not yet plumbed the depths of His suffering. We have yet to consider the one extraordinary event that produced more pain than any other the world would ever know... the solitary incident of blinding, excruciating agony that forever must eclipse all others.

The Most Terrible Scream in History

The celebrated Norwegian painter and printmaker Edvard Munch created a masterpiece of expressionistic art when he put brush to canvas to produce his most famous work, "The Cry." Perhaps you have seen this remarkable painting—a man's face deformed in a spasm of anxiety, the background distorted to echo the circular shape of the cry escaping from the man's mouth. Munch has been called neurotic, but he was a master at depicting the psychological tensions that underlie modern life.[8] "The Cry" portrays emotional pain in a way few of us can ever forget.

Yet as effective as "The Cry" is, it falls infinitely short of depicting the most bloodcurdling cry the world has ever known or ever can know. This was a cry so horrible, so bone-chilling, so frightful that the dead ears of the deaf can still hear its echo thousands of years after it pierced the Palestinian sky. The scream is recorded for us in the pages of the Gospels. And it came from the lips of our Lord as He hung dying on the cross.

> About the ninth hour Jesus cried out in a loud voice, *"Eloi, Eloi, lama sabachthani?"*—which means, "My God, my God, why have you forsaken me?" (Matthew 27:46).

Beyond any doubt, this is the chief cry of pain in the entire Bible. And although Jesus' physical pain was excruciating, it wasn't that which elicited this searing scream. No, the cause of His anguished words was something far darker, far worse, and infinitely more agonizing.

For one mysterious moment, the sinless Lamb of God, the Second Adam who had never tasted even a millisecond of sin, *became sin* on our behalf. In that moment, Jesus' Father, the Holy One of Israel, turned away. His righteous back spoke nothing but silence to the Son. Imagine that if you can. Never had the Father and the Son suffered even the tiniest instant of broken fellowship—and yet now, on the cross, in this unutterably dreadful moment, the Father turned away from the Son as all the vileness of humanity's black corruption and sin cemented itself to the pure, unstained soul of Jesus.

And the Savior let loose The Cry.

Isaiah saw it all hundreds of years before it happened. As his startled eyes focused on the shocking scene before him, he wrote of Jesus, "He was despised and rejected by men, a man of sorrows, and familiar with suffering. . . . Surely he took up our infirmities and carried our sorrows, yet we considered him stricken by God, smitten by him, and afflicted" (Isaiah 53:3-4).

This is how Jesus chose to identify with our suffering. He became a man; He suffered; and therefore with great conviction He can say that He understands us. That is why the writer of Hebrews says,

> Both the one who makes men holy and those who are made holy are of the same family. So Jesus is not ashamed to call them brothers. ...he had to be made like his brothers in every way, in order that he might become a merciful and faithful high priest in service to God, and that he might make atonement for the sins of the people. Because he himself suffered when he was tempted, he is able to help those who are being tempted (Hebrews 2:11,17-18).

God has constructed a great bridge between us and Himself.

Because of Jesus' identification with us, we have a solid basis for trusting that He can heal our sorrows. He pardons not only our sins, but He also removes the sting of other people's sins against us. He frees us from bitterness, resentment, deep feelings of rejection, and inferiority. He replaces them with His Spirit living within us, who convinces us that we are His—that we are cleansed and made whole, pardoned, and given a new relationship with God.

Chapter 53 of Isaiah is a special part of the book dedicated to describing the ministry of a man called the Suffering Servant. Today we know this man as Jesus. Somehow, there is something about His suffering that is very comforting to us—we know that we are not alone. This is the same theme the apostle John picks up in Revelation when he points to the Lamb of God and reminds the saints that Christ went through everything they went through. Jesus is worthy of our worship because of His unblemished character and holy nature, but it is all the easier for us to trust Him when we know He has traveled the same road of pain that we have. We know He has true spiritual authority—an authority rooted not only in who He is, but in what He has done for us by suffering on our behalf. This gives us great confidence to trust Him.

And what was the purpose behind this? Isaiah 53:11 says, "After the suffering of his soul, he will see the light of life and be satisfied; by his knowledge my righteous servant will justify many, and he will bear their iniquities."

Jesus' pain was the gateway to our spiritual health. Before that could happen, however, it was necessary for Him to become a sacrifice. Before the resurrection came the crucifixion. And before the shout of triumph came the scream of pain.

Ancient Greek sculptors were in the habit of tearing out the nails from their thumbs and fingers and not allowing the nails to grow back.[9] They knew the skin underneath the absent nails was extremely sensitive to touch, so when they were working on a piece of art, they would rub that sensitive skin over their work to detect any slight flaw. In this way they would instantly know if the marble was smooth enough.

In much the same way, God has entered into our pain. Through His own woundedness, He took upon Himself the sins of the world, and by so doing He continues to touch the hearts of all who come to Him by faith.

A God Who Redeems the Pain

Before we leave this chapter, I think it's important for us to remember that God not only *feels* our pain, He *redeems* our pain.

This doesn't mean that He keeps us from difficult experiences; rather, in the midst of those experiences, He gives us grace to endure and strength to overcome. As we respond courageously and with trust, *He works within us in such a way that the pain actually becomes worthwhile.* His rewards come in many forms. They may come in changed character, in freedom from sinful flesh patterns, in dependence upon Him that results in deeper intimacy with Him. Or they may come in learning about His character and His ways, in lessons that become part of our life forever.

I can't help but think of Corrie ten Boom. You may remember that Corrie, her sister, and their father used their Dutch home to hide Jews from the Nazis during World War II. She told me some years ago that all her suffering in prison was worth everything she went through in order to save people's lives. But even more than that, it was worth it because of what God did in her heart. She could look back and say it was truly all worthwhile.

Remember, this was a lady thrown into a concentration camp where a number was permanently tattooed on her arm. She saw her sister beaten and killed. She suffered all the privations, all the indignities the Nazis could heap on her. Yet because Corrie was willing to cooperate with the Lord in changing her heart, she became an instrument in God's hands to speak redemption and forgiveness to the Germans. Only a person who had suffered so much could convey the depth of forgiveness and the earnestness of God's offer in such a way that it would speak deeply and powerfully to the souls of the German soldiers.

This is how God redeems a horrible experience and uses it not only in a person, but through that person for the benefit of others.

Corrie came to visit Sally and I on her eightieth birthday when we were living on two houseboats in Amsterdam. She had called and asked to meet with us before she went to America on a speaking trip. Of course I was thrilled with her request and asked if she would speak to our young people. We ran a halfway house (or a halfway boat!) called the Ark, which was filled with about 50 young people—long-haired, hippy-looking kids off the streets. They were former drug addicts, runaways, prostitutes—a pretty scraggly lot. Corrie came to visit, gave her testimony, then asked if we would gather around and pray for her, lay hands on her, and send her as a missionary to America.

I remember marveling at this 80-year-old Dutch "tante" (auntie) who had endured a concentration camp and who was about to speak on television through the Billy Graham crusades. She didn't go to members of Parliament or Dutch Reformed ministers or theologians (which she could easily have done), enjoying ceremonies and inaugurations and big galas. Instead, she just asked a bunch of kids, the broken people of the world, to pray for her! Well, we did pray for her, and as we walked back to her car, she said with a twinkle in her eye, "God has promised me ten more years to live. I've bought new suitcases to celebrate." Aunt Corrie died on her ninetieth birthday, ten years later to the day.

Something deeply puzzled me, however, during the last four-and-a-half years of her life. She spent them bedridden. She suffered one stroke after another, had several heart attacks, and even lost her speech. I went to visit her once with Sally. As we left, I was moved by her suffering. While a light, pleasant, warm spirit had filled the room, nevertheless she was in physical pain. And I asked the Lord, "Why is this? Could you give me some insight into your purposes here?"

A short while later, I felt prompted to turn to 2 Corinthians 4:17: "Our light and momentary troubles are achieving for us an eternal glory that far outweighs them all." And the thought went through my mind: *Perhaps just as Aunt Corrie was prepared through the sufferings of a concentration camp to speak to people all over the world about forgiving their enemies, so now God is preparing her for a new assignment in heaven.*

If only we lived in the light of eternity and saw this present life as an opportunity to redeem difficult experiences and let them become a part of us! There have been several occasions where I felt led to pray to the Lord, "Do anything You want to do; do anything You have to do. I invite You and ask You to do everything You must do so that I will become the person You want me to be."

Don't pray that kind of prayer casually! It's a dangerous prayer; God will take you up on it if you mean business with Him. The answer to that prayer could involve suffering. It certainly will involve testing and purging of everything in our life which keeps us from being all that God wants us to be as instruments of His grace and healing power in other people's lives.

But it will also be so very worthwhile! God is in the business of redeeming our pain.

The royal palace in Teheran, Iran, is breathtaking.[10] When you step into the palace, you are surrounded by millions of pieces of glittering, sparkling glass. It appears as if the domed ceiling, the side walls, and the columns are covered with diamonds. Yet they are not diamonds, but small pieces of mirrors. The edges of the myriad little mirrors refract the light like prisms and throw out all the colors of the rainbow. It is said to be spectacular.

But it was not planned.

When the royal palace was being designed, the architects ordered large mirrors to cover the entrance walls. When the mirrors arrived, it was found they had been broken in transit. Thousands of pieces of smashed mirrors littered the packing crates. The builders were about to dispose of them when one creative man said,

"Perhaps it could be more beautiful because they are broken." He took some of the larger pieces and smashed them also, fitted them together like an abstract mosaic, and fastened them to the walls. Today the palace is beautiful beyond words, awash with sparkling rainbows of color.

In the same way, God takes the broken mirrors of our lives and rearranges them in divinely creative ways to create a mosaic beautiful beyond words. He knows how to redeem our pain. Our job is to let Him do His job.

How Should We Respond to God's Pain?

It is easy to ask questions concerning the pain of God, but if we are to live as His children, we must examine *our response* to evil and suffering. Do we react as deeply as God does to evil in the world and in our own lives? Do we share the sorrow of God's heart over sin and the destruction it brings to all that it touches?

We can never experience complete healing for our emotional wounds or fully receive the Father's love unless we share God's sorrow over sin and selfishness. The Bible teaches there is a difference between godly sorrow and worldly sorrow over sin. Paul wrote to the Corinthian Christians, "Now I am happy, not because you were made sorry, but because your sorrow led you to repentance. For you became sorrowful as God intended and so were not harmed in any way by us. Godly sorrow brings repentance that leads to salvation and leaves no regret, but worldly sorrow brings death" (2 Corinthians 7:9-10).

Our sin has broken God's heart. God, however, has not just grieved over sin; He did something about it. He gave His own Son as a sacrifice to pay for the sins of the world. We deserved to be punished for breaking God's laws, but He sent Jesus to take our place.

How should we respond? We must choose to be more concerned about the pain that God feels in His heart over man's selfishness than about the hurts we feel. By deciding to put God first in our lives, we can break out of the patterns of manipulation, self-pity, or fear that plague us. God the Father yearns to love us as His children and heal us of our hurts, but that cannot happen unless we give Him full control of our lives.

The End of Pain

God knows when we are hurting. In all our afflictions, He too is afflicted. Perhaps that is why He goes out of His way to tell us about a coming day when pain will be no more—when sighing, groaning, and weeping will flee away. He doesn't like pain any more than we do.

Twice in the last book of the Bible—once a little ways from the beginning, once at the end—the Lord makes a point of announcing to us that soon, God will wipe away every tear from our eyes (Revelation 7:17; 21:4).

The book ends on that note. It's what God is leading up to. It's what He was about at the cross. It's a central part of His plan for us. And I don't mind admitting to you that it's a promise I can meditate on all day long.

[God] will wipe every tear from their eyes. There will be no more death or mourning or crying or pain ... (Revelation 21:4).

6

FROM MY HEAD
TO MY HEART

*O*n April 11, 1970, a giant towering more than 360 feet tall and weighing more than 3,000 tons suddenly grew angry. Fire belched from beneath his gargantuan feet as he lurched out of his den and made a headlong dash for a faraway, mysterious kingdom.

Apollo 13 was on its way to the moon.[1]

This was to be no ordinary lunar visit, however. Two days after the launch and some 205,000 miles from earth, Mission Control learned that the lives of the three astronauts were in peril. An explosion in the Service Module had damaged the main power supply and cut off the only source of oxygen for the crew. There was only one hope for survival: The men would have to use the Lunar Module as a "lifeboat." With little heat and less room, the men wedged themselves into the LM, continued on their quarter-of-a-million-mile journey to the moon, used its gravitational pull to whip them hurtling back home, then just before reentry, crawled back into the Command Module. Six days after the most harrowing flight in the history of the U.S. space program, Apollo 13 splashed down safely in the Pacific Ocean.

Investigators, of course, clamored to know what had gone wrong. What incredible force had almost fatally wounded this state-of-the-art space vehicle longer than a football field and weighing more than six million pounds? Answer: an ordinary oxygen tank, impossibly small in comparison to the mammoth Saturn V rocket that launched Apollo 13 into space.

For Want of a Nail

What's the old saying? "For want of a nail, the shoe was lost; for want of a shoe, the horse was lost; and for want of a horse, the rider was lost." In 1970, for want of a small oxygen tank, the mission—and the lives of three men—was almost lost.

It's amazing, isn't it? The "want of" the tiniest things can make all the difference between success and failure, jubilation and sorrow, and even life and death. Small doesn't necessarily mean insignificant. Sometimes the strength of a chain depends on its weakest links.

That's exactly the case with this chapter of *The Healing Power of Love*. It's one of the shorter chapters in the book—but don't suppose that makes it insignificant! In some ways, it's the most important chapter you'll read. In fact, if you and I fail to connect here, all could be lost. Like the saying "for want of a nail..." the reader could be lost.

I don't want that to happen; I don't want to lose you. I want you on a good horse, confidently riding on solid ground, all four hooves protected by rugged shoes firmly and securely attached. That takes some good nails.

So with that in mind, I think it's time to drive the first nail.

Nail #1

Becky Pippert, author of *Out of the Saltshaker and into the World,* was speaking many years ago at a conference in Portland, Oregon. She began her talk with this: "Wherever I go, one of the persistent questions Christians ask is this: *'Why am I not farther along?'* " That question reflects almost a kind of quiet despair. We see the biblical promises and we know they are true, yet we're not as far along as we know we ought to be. We didn't know life was going to be as difficult as it is. So whose fault is it? Is it my fault? Do my problems mock faith?

I doubt there is a single believer who listens to the current revelations on Christian TV and doesn't feel, "O God, just give me the grace to live what I believe! Help my insides to match my outsides!"

That's the real challenge for all of us, isn't it? To get our insides to match our outsides. To line up our professed beliefs with our actions. How do we get what we believe in our heads to take up residence in our hearts in such a way that it radically affects the way we live?

I once asked a friend, "Why is it that Christians don't grow when they believe all the right stuff and really want to grow?" He looked at me for a moment, paused, then said thoughtfully, "Floyd, it's because they haven't truly had a revelation of who they are "in Christ."

My friend then turned to Ephesians chapter 1. He pointed out the apostle's words: "I keep asking that the God of our Lord Jesus Christ, the glorious Father, may *give you the Spirit of wisdom and revelation.* . . . I pray also that the *eyes of your heart may be enlightened*" (verses 17-18).

The apostle asked his heavenly Father to give the Ephesians *revelation.* What kind? The kind that would allow them to know who they really were. He asked that the eyes of their heart would be enlightened so that they could *know!*

My friend looked me in the eye and, with regret in his voice, contended that this crucial prayer is missing from the experience of far too many of us. Although Paul thought it necessary to pray that God would reveal the tremendous truth of their new identity to his Christian brothers and sisters, somehow we don't think it necessary to pray the same prayer. My friend also noted that Paul made this request on behalf of men and women who had already come to Christ. Paul was praying for believers, not unbelievers. His prayer was aimed at securing spiritual revelation for believers so they would know who they had become and what they had received in Christ.

So why don't people grow even when they want to? It's because they have never had a revelation by the Holy Spirit in which He conveys to their heart that they are, indeed, His. This isn't a "revelation" like that received by the prophets and apostles who wrote the Bible; the revelation that is needed is a divine application of biblical truth to our hearts—the Holy Spirit's personal confirmation to each of us, individually, that we have truly been made a new person. The revelation we need—and for which Paul prayed—is a deep, unshakeable conviction from the Spirit of God that we have been made a new person with a new identity.

This is crucial because you act like who you think you are. Do you see yourself as a victorious Christian? One who has everything it takes to fulfill every longing of your heart? *You will live like who you think you are!*

A Christian is not merely someone who *gets* something... whether it is forgiveness, the Holy Spirit, a new beginning, a new nature, or whatever else we might be thankful for receiving. *A Christian is a new person—* someone he was not before. This is not just a position we have, nor is it a way God sees us through the blood of Christ. It is actually who we have become! This is true whether you feel like it or not, whether you believe it or not, whether you act like it or not. You have become His child.

If you have received Jesus as your Lord and Savior, you are a different person. You may wear the same clothes, weigh the same, and still like the same food— but you are not the same. You have been changed on the inside. You are now in the Father's family. You have been adopted. Sometimes it takes time to believe that is true, but it is!

129

Nail #2

Over the years I've counseled scores of people who in their minds knew this truth, but who in their hearts couldn't seem to embrace it. They were not able to connect their heart with their head. They had not received a personal revelation that they were indeed a new person.

Oh, they knew all about justification by faith. They could tell you that God accepts them not based on their performance, but because Jesus died in their place on the cross. They would insist that Christ is their atoning sacrifice, that God has done everything necessary for them to be forgiven, and that faith is the key to it all—but somehow they never *emotionally* took hold of it.

I believe these folks not only haven't received a revelation of who they are in Christ, but they also have failed to follow the apostle Paul's example as laid out in Philippians 3:12, where he wrote, "I press on to take hold of that for which Christ Jesus took hold of me." Did you catch what Paul said? He claimed he had been "taken hold of" by Jesus Christ. The Savior had reached out to him in love, snatched him from the evil one, and brought him into the kingdom of light one glorious afternoon on a dusty road outside of Damascus. How wonderful! Yet Paul said there was still something left for him to do—something that God did not do for him. It was Paul's job to "take hold" of that which had already taken hold of him. What does that mean?

We've been seized by God, Paul says, but to seize God ourselves . . . that's something else again. It's as if

God has given us a big bear hug. To make the hug emotionally satisfying (not to make it a reality; His arms are already around us!), we must wrap our own weak and trembling arms around Him. The best hugs have to go both ways.

Maybe an illustration will help. John MacArthur tells about a pastor friend who was conducting a series of meetings in several churches in the Carolinas.[2] The man was staying in the home of some friends and traveled from there to the various places he was speaking.

One evening he was scheduled to speak in a church several hours away. Some other friends offered to pick him up and return him after the meeting. The man told his hosts he'd be back sometime around midnight.

When he returned, he saw the porch light on and assumed his hosts would be ready for him. He told his driver to return home, saying, "You must hurry. You have a long drive back. I'm sure they're prepared for me; I'll have no problem."

It was winter and bitterly cold. By the time he reached the porch, his nose and ears were already numb. He knocked softly but no one answered. He knocked harder and harder, but got no response. Finally he began to beat on the kitchen door and a side window, but no one answered.

At last he decided to find a telephone booth so he could call his hosts. Since he didn't know the area and it was dark, he ended up walking several miles. During his search he slipped on some wet grass and slid down a bank into two feet of icy water. Soaked and nearly frozen, he crawled back to the road and walked until he saw a motel. He woke up the manager, who graciously let him use the phone.

"I hate to disturb you," the man said to his host through chattering teeth, "but I couldn't get anyone in the house to wake up. I'm several miles down the road at the motel. Could you come and get me?"

"My dear friend," replied his host, "you have a key in your overcoat pocket. Don't you remember? I gave it to you before you left." The man checked his coat, and there was the key. He had the ability to enter the house all along!

How like that man we often are. We try to heal our hurts through purely human means, not realizing that all the while we possess Christ, who is the key to every cure. We have the key; we must simply use it. We have been seized by God; now we must seize Him in return. *Taking hold of Jesus is not a matter of what you do, but receiving the inheritance we have been given in Christ.*

The crucial question is, how do we receive this wonderful gift? What does it mean to take the key out of our pockets and use it? How do we take hold of that which has taken hold of us?

Nail #3

God is the one who wants His children to rest secure in the knowledge that they belong to Him. It was His idea. If you have committed your life to Christ through faith, believing that He died for your sins on the cross and was raised to life by His Father three days later, then, according to Scripture, you are God's child.

Many people believe what I have just written; their problem is they just can't seem to *embrace* it. It seems to them like a true fairy tale, if you can imagine such a thing—an impossible story with an impossibly happy ending that is supposed to have truly happened. They believe the words on the page, but the words seem true only on the page of the book and not on the pages of their life.

That's why I'm glad God didn't announce this great, good news on the pages of the Book alone (as wonderful as that is). According to Romans 8:16, He's writing these glorious words—in His own handwriting!—on our very spirits: "The Spirit himself testifies with our spirit that we are God's children."

Romans 8:16 is an ironclad promise from God to us. It guarantees that head knowledge of salvation will work its way down deep into our hearts... into the very core of our beings. This verse pledges to us that, as infinitely precious as are the Bible's written assurances of our salvation, the Spirit Himself has vowed to *personally, deliberately, continually,* and *directly* convince our own spirits that we are His and He is ours!

Nail #4

The word of God says, "...whenever our hearts condemn us....God is greater than our hearts..." (1 John 3:20).

Notice John says, "*Whenever* our hearts condemn us" not "*If* our hearts condemn us." There are no "ifs" about it. John knows Satan will attack, and he knows his attack will come at our most vital and vulnerable

133

point. *There is no more vital point than our confidence in God's love for us.* Make no mistake about it: The devil *will* try to convince you that you've blown it, that there's no hope for you, that you're a castaway, and that God couldn't possibly have made you a part of His holy family. It *will* happen. Perhaps it's happening right now.

Because of that devilish certainty, John focuses our attention on God's love: "God is greater than our hearts, and he knows everything" (verse 20). There's nothing you can do that will surprise God! And even if your heart whispers that you are lost, God Himself shouts back that you have been found—and He never loses what He finds! It's as if the apostle has bracketed this pivotal lesson between two marvelous bookends, both of which are marked, "God's amazing love."

If John were teaching a seminar at a Bible conference today, he would probably say,

1. You will blow it;

2. The devil will jump all over you even if you don't blow it;

3. God's love is greater.

He would end by saying, "I want to teach you a simple yet profound truth. There is nothing you can ever do to make God stop loving you. He loves you because He loves you! *God is love!*"

Nail #5

Paul, too, knew the absolute necessity of getting our heart to agree with our head in embracing God's love for us. That is why he wrote in Romans 5:17 "...those who receive God's abundant provision of grace and of the gift of righteousness [will] reign in life."

He's saying that if you want this great truth to go deep into your heart and not just into your brain, you need to receive it from God by faith. *In the simple act of receiving God's love by faith we grow in our faith.* It is an act of obedience that results in greater faith. I sometimes receive God's love by praying a simple, childlike prayer like this:

> Lord, I'm feeling insecure right now. I need your love. You have promised it to me, so I receive it from you by faith. I don't feel loved, Lord Jesus, but I choose to believe your word. I receive who you are. You are everything I need. You are my confidence, Lord Jesus. You are my security. You are my self-worth. You are in me and I am in you. Thank you, Lord, for making me a new person. I am yours and by faith I trust from this moment on I will experience your love in a new way.

Putting the Shoes On

What I've just written suggests that laying hold of the promise of Romans 8:16 doesn't always happen automatically. Sometimes God in His sovereignty chooses to do a special work in a man or woman's heart, and in a flash and for all time convinces him or her of this marvelous truth. But for most of us, it doesn't happen that way. It takes some Holy Spirit-aided effort—not a work of the flesh, but what the Bible would call "the obedience of faith" to enable us to "take hold of that for which Christ Jesus took hold of us."

Perhaps we could think of it this way: When our family lived in Amsterdam, my children Misha and Matthew learned to speak Dutch like natives. They didn't want to sound like Americans. But acquiring Dutch didn't "just happen." They grew into the language. It took:

1. *Time.* You don't learn a new language overnight. It takes weeks, months, or even years.

2. *Receiving instruction and correction.* What would have happened if Misha or Matthew had studied the wrong lessons? What if they spent years studying Spanish in order to learn Dutch? If they approached a vendor in Amsterdam and asked confidently, "¿Habla usted, Espanol?" they would have looked silly. If the lessons are wrong, the time you spend studying them leads only to frustration. Matthew and Misha picked up Dutch by being with Dutch children, and by hearing and practicing the language. They learned to speak it properly with the help of a Dutch teacher who corrected their mistakes and taught them good grammar.

3. *Practice.* The only way to learn a language inside-out is to speak it. There's no substitute for practice. When you make mistakes, you try again. You work at it and then work at it some more.

4. *Listening to native speakers.* You can learn a lot about a language from books, but there's nothing like hearing native speakers. You watch them, listen to them, study them, and then imitate what they say.

5. *Humility to make mistakes in front of others.* We have to step out and say the difficult sounds we are learning. That means speaking up even though other people may burst out laughing the first time they hear us try to speak the language. Learning to speak a language requires humility.

When you combine these five elements on a consistent basis, there will come a day when you find your tongue fluently spitting out words, phrases, sentences, and even complex thoughts in a language you formerly thought of as "foreign." But it's foreign no longer; now it's a part of you.

Misha found out there was a huge difference between knowing Dutch in her head and having it become a part of her. I still remember the time when she realized the language had become a part of who she was. It happened on the night when she first dreamed in Dutch.

In one sense, to really learn Dutch, Misha had to be "born again." She committed herself to being Dutch. Misha wanted something badly enough to pay the price to get it, and in this case the price was absorption in Dutch culture. It was a passion for her, an unwavering desire expressed in an unfaltering commitment. And eventually she was rewarded with the happy gift of fluent Dutch!

Do you realize that, sometimes, the more precious the gift, the more you have to pay for it? We unwisely believe at times that if it's a gift from God, it should come on a silver platter, wrapped in pretty paper with a bow on top. We want to open it up and there it is: Character! Love! Patience! But often it takes more than that.

To receive something by faith requires action and humility on our part. *Faith is not passively sitting around waiting for God to do something to you.*

I think that's true for most of us who want to get the truth of our new identity from our head into our heart. We have God's promise that it's possible; we have His assurance that it's His great desire; and we have His instruction that it's within our grasp. The key question is this: Are we ready to receive the truth by faith and then live out what we have received?

This issue of our identity is fundamental to who we are. Yet it is also a mystery. We have been so programmed to perform, we have spent so many years hiding and protecting ourselves, that we have to learn a whole new way of *being*. Not doing, but being.

I have found that this kind of *being* often takes the five commitments similar to those Matthew and Misha had in their endeavors to learn Dutch:

1. *Time.* If you're one of the blessed ones who has never struggled for a moment with doubting God's love for you, give thanks. But if it is a struggle for you, remember that such sweet

assurance often builds over time. It builds as you give thanks for it and receive it by faith. The longer you know Him, the more your heart will shout, "Amen!" to your head.

2. *Receiving the truth.* Some of us struggle with God's acceptance because we're not studying the correct materials. We're listening to "internal tapes" that warn us we have to measure up to receive God's love. Some of us are reading books that insist the key to spiritual growth is trying harder, giving more, fasting more, praying more. And what's the inevitable result? Frustration. God's Word encourages us to believe in a God of fathomless love who reached out to us in all our sin through the cross of Christ. He's still reaching out today, waiting for us to receive His grace in abundance.

3. *Practice.* If we really want our heart to embrace the truth our mind has believed, then we need to practice what God asks us to practice. That is, we continually remind ourselves of His love for us and we constantly look for ways to share His love with others.

4. *Listening.* Do you know anyone who, for many years, has seemed to bask in the love of God? Spend time with men and women like that. Watch them. Listen to them. Imitate them. And you'll find that you'll become a lot like them. Listen to God with them. Pray with them. Read the Word with them. And your heart will fall in love with our Father in heaven.

5. *Humility.* You can never learn a language unless you are willing to look or sound a little foolish. It takes genuine humility to learn to speak a foreign tongue. And so it is with growing in the revelation of who we are in Christ. We must acknowledge our need to receive this revelation and be open about any flesh patterns that hold us back from receiving the truth of who we really are. Unless we are willing to be accountable through transparency, as frightening as that may be, we will not be able to receive this revelation to our hearts. Go ahead—take the step. Call sin sin, ask for help, and watch yourself grow!

Now Ride!

A poem by James Whitcomb Riley describes the death of a shop worker. He says that as the workmen stood around on the day of the man's funeral and talked about their departed mate and friend, one teary-eyed man declared, "When God made him, I bet He didn't do anything else that day but jest sat around and felt good."[3]

The truth is, that's the way God feels about *all* of us, whether we feel it or not. God does love you... more than you'll ever fully grasp. And it's His great desire that a growing knowledge of His love for you will so grip your mind and your heart that you'll rest secure in that love, no matter what hardships or hurts or difficulties come your way.

Such is the healing power of love.

Therefore we do not lose heart. Though outwardly we are wasting away, yet inwardly we are being renewed day by day. For our light and momentary troubles are achieving for us an eternal glory that far outweighs them all. So we fix our eyes not on what is seen, but on what is unseen. For what is seen is temporary, but what is unseen is eternal (2 Corinthians 4:16-18).

And, I might add, *unbelievably good!*

7

THE HEALING POWER OF LOVE

*S*everal years ago a woman approached Becky Pippert after a speaking engagement.[1] Becky describes
the woman as "lovely, godly—and utterly tortured." The
woman kept sobbing and could hardly get out her story.
Finally, she began to describe how, many years earlier, she
and her husband (who was then her fiancé) were youth
leaders in a conservative, evangelical church. They were
scheduled to get married in July, but before their wedding
they slept together and she became pregnant. The thought
of what this would do to the church was more than the
woman could handle; she knew her church just couldn't
cope. But she also knew it was her own pride that she
couldn't handle. Here they were, counseling the church's
young people, and yet they were not role models themselves. The couple never told anyone about the pregnancy.
Instead, they got an abortion.

"Becky," she sobbed, "I believe with all of my heart
that I have murdered an innocent life. We have had a

wonderful marriage, been involved in ministry, and have four darling children. But I live every day with the guilt that I have killed a life. I don't know how I ever could have killed an innocent child . . ."

As Becky listened to the woman's agony and saw her torture, a thought crossed her mind. But she brushed it off and said nothing, thinking it could not be from God. *If I said that to her,* thought Becky, *it would destroy her.* Meanwhile the woman continued her tearful confession: "Becky, I cannot believe I could have killed an innocent one."

After listening awhile longer, Becky finally stopped the woman. Hoping that what she was about to say was from God, Becky replied, "I don't know why you are so surprised. Because this isn't your first murder; it's your second."

The woman abruptly went silent and looked at Becky, aghast. Becky continued.

"The cross shows all of us are crucifiers. Aborters or nonaborters, religious or irreligious. All of us are revealed as crucifiers when we look at the cross. We have all participated, killing the only innocent life there ever was. Our sins are precisely what drove Him there. And yet you seem surprised that you could kill your own child, when you have already killed God's Child."

As the speechless woman stared at Becky, a new thought clearly began dawning in her startled consciousness. "That's true," she finally whispered. "You're right. I have, in fact, felt more guilty over killing my own son than in killing God's. You're saying that I have done something even worse than what I am confessing.

146

Before today, I couldn't imagine anything worse than what I did. But you are telling me the cross shows me I'm even worse than I thought!"

The woman paused for a moment, deep in thought, then went on, "If I am even worse than what I thought, what you are saying is that the worst thing I have done is already forgiven, is that right? You're saying that the cross shows me that the worst evil in the world has been absorbed and forgiven! And if that has been forgiven, how can my confession of this sin *not* be forgiven?"

At that moment, this tortured woman smiled at Becky, began to weep for joy, and exclaimed, "Oh Becky—talk about amazing grace!"

"That day," Becky said of this incident, "I saw someone walk right into the heart and mystery of the cross. I saw someone literally transformed by a proper understanding of Calvary. It happened only when she took her sin and pain to the cross, a cross that insists on highlighting our evil in order to leave us absolutely no doubt that we have been forgiven. That woman intuitively recognized that God works according to the deepest psychological law of acceptance: that for us to really believe we are accepted, we must know that we have been accepted at our very worst. That is precisely what the cross does, and that is why we can face the reality of our sin, because God's solution is so wonderful. That is what gives us the confidence to be unafraid. We come to the cross and realize that there is no one who will ever love us like Jesus."

Do you believe that? That no one will ever love us like Jesus? What powerful words these are! And what marvelous truth! *We are getting close to the very heart of love's healing power.* But before we explore the precious mother lode itself, it might be good for us to take a moment and consider why we need God's healing love in the first place.

The Hunger for Healing Begins

Throughout this book we have been talking about the healing power of love. But where did the hunger for healing begin? What prompted it?

To get to the roots of the story we have to go all the way back to Adam and Eve. Before sin ever stained humankind, Adam and Eve were magnificent beings, the crowning achievement of God's work. Unlike any of His other creations, Adam and Eve were made in God's image, in His likeness. Nothing in all the universe compared to them. They were simply breathtaking.

Psalm 8 gives us a glimpse of how spectacular this first couple was. In nine short verses, David meditates over God's wondrous creature, man. In verse five he uses a Hebrew term to describe man and woman that's so shocking, so sensational, most Bible translations to this day won't render the phrase literally. The NIV, for example, reads, "You made him [humankind] a little lower than *the heavenly beings* and crowned him with glory and honor," while both The Living Bible and the King James translate the phrase "a little lower than the angels." But the phrase in Hebrew is neither "heavenly beings" or "angels." It's something vastly superior to either of these; it's the word *Elohim*, one of the names of God. So the phrase literally reads, "You made him a little lower than *God.* ..."

As I said, scandalous!

But that's the Bible's own evaluation of human-kind—"little lower than God." Adam and his wife were given authority over the entire earth and for a time they reigned together as God's co-regents on this planet.

Unfortunately, that idyllic scene didn't last. When Adam joined his wife in disobedience, they lost much of their glory and forfeited open communion with God. Their rebellion and sin led to further actions of disobedience, which resulted in a new emotion: paralyzing fear. They knew they were guilty and a deep sense of shame and condemnation swept over them. When God called out to the man, "Adam, where are you?" He found His chief creation cowering in the bushes, vainly trying to cover his shame.

Since that dismal day, all of us have repeated this sad scene. Each of us has ratified Adam's rebellion and discovered the horrifying power of shame. And as we've noted earlier, if we don't go to God to deal with the resulting guilt and shame of our sin, we will follow Adam's futile route: We'll run from God and vainly try to hide from Him.

Yet we can never be restored if we're running and hiding. Sin wounds us, whether it's our sin or someone else's. And if we try to heal ourselves with some fig-leaf remedy, if we set up a pharmacy in our garden and try to concoct some herbs to salve our wounds, if we join the French Foreign Legion to run away to some distant shore, we will never find the healing we so desperately seek.

The good news is that God already has done everything He needs to do to bring us back to full health. The work of Jesus Christ on the cross has won for us complete freedom from sin, guilt, and shame. Because of what Jesus did for us at Calvary, we don't have to run or hide.

As Becky Pippert told the young woman, however, we can never receive the forgiveness of Christ if we don't first believe we're guilty. The irony of the cross is that you have to admit you're guilty—that *you* crucified Jesus, that *you* should have been the sacrifice up there instead of Him—or you will never be free of guilt. Martin Luther said, "We carry His very nails in our pockets." Until we fully come to grips with the awfulness of our sin, the cross of Christ and the forgiveness He offers will never fully impact our life.

We might say that forgiveness is directly related to acknowledgment of guilt. That's why Jesus said to the Pharisees, "It is not the healthy who need a doctor, but the sick. I have not come to call the righteous, but sinners to repentance" (Luke 5:31-32). In other words, "Gentlemen, if you don't think you're sick, I can't help you get well. The only people who get cured are the ones who admit they are consumed by a fatal disease."

If we want to enjoy the healing power of God's love, we have to acknowledge our *sin*—not just our hurt, but our sin. Our sin is terrible, incomprehensible, hideous. All of us, like the woman who came to Becky, must come to the place where we say, "The cross shows me that I have done more than fail God. It is not just that others have sinned against me, a victim. I really am worse than I thought."

We're Worse than We Thought

I believe this truth is behind the apostle Paul's many expressions of personal guilt, which we find in his letters:

- ✦ I am the least of the apostles and do not even deserve to be called an apostle, because I persecuted the church of God (1 Corinthians 15:9).

- ✦ You have heard of my previous way of life in Judaism, how intensely I persecuted the church of God and tried to destroy it (Galatians 1:13).

- ✦ I am unspiritual, sold as a slave to sin. I do not understand what I do. For what I want to do I do not do, but what I hate I do (Romans 7:14-15).

- ✦ What a wretched man I am! Who will rescue me from this body of death? (Romans 7:24).

Paul's chief confession, however, is found in 1 Timothy 1:15, where he says, "Christ Jesus came into the world to save sinners—of whom I am the worst." Paul had no difficulty admitting his sin. Even toward the end of his days, the illustrious apostle could look at his life and say, "Guilty" without groveling or going into a "pity party."

Yet he didn't stop there (and we must not either)! Paul was no devotee of worm theology. He didn't wallow in his sin and he didn't allow it to break his spirit. In verse 16 he immediately adds, "But for that very reason I was shown mercy so that in me, the worst of sinners, Christ Jesus might display his unlimited patience as an example for those who would believe on him and receive eternal life."

Because of God's grace, Paul was able to say, "I really am worse than I thought. So are you! So are we all! We don't have any idea how guilty we really are, apart from Christ. But, thank God, it doesn't stop there. God has done a miracle in my life to make me a new man. In fact, He gave me a name change—from Saul to Paul—to signify the radical transformation He brought about in me. And He can make the same change in you!"

He really can! If we could just begin to grasp and embrace three foundational truths of the gospel, our emotional healing would be secured forever.

Justified in Christ

The very heart of love's healing power is found beating on a Roman cross and in a Jewish tomb. Our ultimate emotional healing was won for us through the death and resurrection of Jesus Christ. Paul wrote:

> Righteousness from God comes through faith in Jesus Christ to all who believe. There is no difference, for all have sinned and fall short of the glory of God, and are justified freely by his grace through the redemption that came by Christ Jesus (Romans 3:22-24).

The key word in this passage (in a passage chock-full of key words!) is "justified." When Paul says we are justified, he means that God has forgiven all our sins, pardoned us from the consequences of sin (it is one thing to be forgiven, but He also pardons us—sets us free!), and has adopted us into His heart of love. He has made us His own. We were rebellious, prison-bound sinners and became forgiven, accepted children of God. We have a whole new standing in life all because of what Jesus did on our behalf. God freely grants all this to us when, in simple faith, we accept this offer of love through His Son, Jesus Christ.

Oh, if only we could begin to understand and embrace the riches that are ours because God has justified us by His grace! If only we could catch a glimmer of what has been lavished upon us in Christ! If only our hearts would wrap arms of faith around God's precious promises! Then, at last, we would begin to fully experience the healing power of love.

Paul never could get over how wonderful this news was. The delight, relief, and surprise of it stayed with him throughout his life. You can almost hear his excitement when he writes to the Romans, "God demonstrates his own love for us in this: While we were still sinners, Christ died for us. Since we have now been justified by his blood, how much more shall we be saved from God's wrath through him!" (Romans 5:8-9). The certainty that Jesus died and rose again changed everything for Paul—and it changes everything for us as well. It changes the way we see ourselves, how we treat each other, the kind of children we rear, the way we look at marriage, the way we spend money, and much, much more. Jesus' death and resurrection form the very foundation for our understanding of who we most deeply are.

The fact that we crucified Him and yet have been forgiven means there is nothing we can ever do that is worse than that! If God forgave us of that, then there is nothing we can ever do, no matter how discouraged we become because of our miscues or hardships or struggles—nothing, absolutely nothing can separate us from the love of Christ... nothing!

But there is a second part to this good news. Not only did we crucify Him, the Bible also says we were crucified *with Him*. "I have been crucified with Christ and I no longer live, but Christ lives in me," Paul wrote. "The life I live in the body, I live by faith in the Son of God, who loved me and gave himself for me" (Galatians 2:20). This is an astonishing claim. Paul says, "I have the greatest news for you: You are dead!"

Some people might be tempted to think Paul was depressed the day he wrote that. "The poor boy should have listened to a good, positive-thinking tape that day," they might suggest. But Paul was not depressed. Paul would say, "If only you knew what it means that you died, you would stand to your feet and sing the Hallelujah Chorus! If only you grasped what it is that died in you!"

What is it that died in us? Sin's authority to dominate us. Paul insists that evil's power to rule us has been crushed. That means we don't have to live under neurotic compulsions and anxieties and sins anymore;

we don't have to allow our pain and hurts to dictate how we live.

Christ has solved the problem of sin—not merely the individual incidents of sin in my life, but the root of the problem. It's total coverage. Paul tells us we must come to understand that our rebellious spirit has been broken and we have been forgiven—so get on with the new life! If we have been justified through faith in Christ, a new day has dawned. And what a glorious day it is!

A Totally New Person

It is wonderful beyond words to know that God has forgiven all of our sins and made us righteous—totally acceptable to the Father. He has restored to us the glory that was lost in the Garden of Eden when Adam and Eve sinned. Now if that were all that happened to us when we became Christians, it would be enough to shout about for all eternity. But being the kind of loving God He is, our Lord wasn't satisfied with that. He decided not only to pardon us from sin, but also to make us into new people—not merely to slap a fresh coat of paint on an old model. In theological terms, we were not only justified but *regenerated*.

Justification brought about a change in our relationship to God (from enemies to friends); regeneration brought a complete change in our moral and spiritual nature (from depraved to holy). We needed to be justified because we were guilty; we needed to be regenerated because we were dirty.

We are totally new people, and God says we are

holy, pure, and spotless. Not because He somehow chooses to see us that way (even though it isn't really true), but because *He really made us into this new kind of human being!* He imparts to us His Spirit, and in giving us this gift of Himself, He transforms us to become His children. He cleans us up. Like a child who is dirty from playing outside and needs a bath, He bathes us. He washes everything off of us—inside and out. All the perversions, all the filth, all the hate, all the anger—everything is washed away.

We are a "new creation; the old has gone, the new has come!" according to Paul (2 Corinthians 5:17). We have been "born of God," according to John (1 John 5:1).

Or, as Paul tells us, "He saved us through the washing of rebirth and renewal by the Holy Spirit, whom he poured out on us generously through Jesus Christ our Savior, so that, having been justified by his grace, we might become heirs having the hope of eternal life" (Titus 3:5-7).

If you are a believer in Jesus, you are a brand-new creation!

David Needham provides an excellent illustration that can help us picture what this means.[2] Imagine that you entered this world as a crab apple tree. This is the kind of tree you were by nature as a result of repeated disobedience to God (*see* Ephesians 2:3).

But then one day a momentous event took place. Someone took a knife and made a long, diagonal cut across your trunk and sliced off the entire top of you. Almost immediately this same person took a fresh, green section of stem, cut with a matching diagonal slice from a different tree, and spliced it onto what was left of you. The splice was carefully wrapped and sealed, and a tag was attached to you that read, "Golden Delicious."

Soon afterward the buds above that splice began to burst with life. And what would those blossoms produce? Crab apples? No way! Whoever takes a bite out of that fruit will get a mouthful of sweet, tasty, golden delicious apples. Why? *Because that is who you now are.* Needham writes, "No one who knew what had taken place would ever think of calling you a 'crab apple.' You are not even a crab apple + a golden delicious. You *are* a 'golden delicious.' "[3]

In the same way, when God regenerated you, He made you into a new person. You are not part sinner and part saint; you are all saint. Your new identity is golden delicious, not crab apple.

But isn't it still possible for us to sin? Sure it is. But when we do, we do so *against our nature.*

Back to Needham's illustration: If a gardener is not careful to prune away the growth below the graft, the trunk will sprout crab apples. Gardeners call these sprouts "suckers." These suckers are considered usurpers and aliens, worthy only of removal. They no longer represent what the tree is now. Needham tells us:

> The moment you were born again, the unregenerate person you used to be—your "old self" (crab apple)—was sliced off—"crucified." That which you had been by nature, "a child of wrath," you are no more. There it

157

lies on the ground, dead. At this same moment (the . . . grafting moment) you became
a genuine "new self," a golden delicious.[4]

Yes, it is still possible for you to sin, just as it is
possible for a grafted tree to produce bad fruit. That's
why a gardener has to be vigilant about pruning below
the graft. It's also why we must be vigilant to "put to
death, therefore, whatever belongs to your earthly nature: sexual immorality, impurity, lust, evil desires and
greed, which is idolatry" (Colossians 3:5).

Needham's personal testimony about his discovery
is so compelling I'd like to excerpt part of it for you in
case you are struggling with the same issues that troubled him:

As a young Christian, I still assumed I was a
crab apple—a forgiven crab apple. Therefore,
not realizing that God had performed such a
radical grafting act upon me, I had no idea
that I was a new person—golden delicious.

Because of that ignorance, I believed that
"crab apple" growth *was what I was.* No matter
how many branches I chopped off, they came
right back. I tried "dying to self" dozens of
times. But the sap had to flow somewhere. To
me, they weren't "alien suckers." They were
who I was and nothing else. What could I do?

Since I had my well-developed list of the
proper "do's" and "don'ts" of Christian behavior, I became an expert at attaching imitation

golden delicious fruit to my chopped-back crab apple branches. I imagine that, at times, I was so successful other people assumed what they saw was the real thing.

Then came an enlightening thought. Instead of imitation apples, what God was after was the real thing—the "fruit of the Spirit." Because his fruit would be alien to crab apple trees, it would require a major step of faith to trust him to hang his "golden delicious" fruit on my gnarly, half-pruned crab apple branches. This is the way I saw myself—sort of like a "Peanuts" cartoon Christmas tree.[5]

Until he discovered the truth of regeneration! Then at last Needham came to see that

"sinning (crab apple producing) is so utterly irrational—so stupid—*no one in their right mind would ever consider sinning a reasonable or natural behavior.* In other words, it is as unthinkable for a Christian to sin as it is for a golden delicious apple tree to produce crab apples (even though that is still possible below the graft...).

I wonder what effect it would have upon us if we realized that every time we chose to sin, we were choosing to act as *temporarily insane?* I would be the first to admit such times. But how stupid! That's exactly what any nurseryman would think about me—every time I would choose to let a sucker grow on my golden delicious tree. Why? Because I would be choosing to frustrate the true nature of that tree. 'Crazy,' they would say, and rightly so."[6]

When we were regenerated, we were transformed—changed into new people. Yet somehow, for most of us, it seems far easier to believe that Jesus died and rose again than to believe that *we* died and were raised to new life with Him.

Oh, we may say we understand and believe that we have become new people, but sometimes I wonder. When we find ourselves at a social gathering where we feel ill at ease, what do we do? When we say something foolish or do something stupid, what do we think? What goes through our mind at a moment like that? Or suppose someone says or does something that triggers old emotions, which, in turn, brings up old lies: "I'm a failure. No one could love me if they really knew what I was like." Do we say to ourselves, "I am such a turkey. I am always acting like an idiot. This is so embarrassing." Or do we say, "My, this is remarkable—that a member of royalty could act so out of character!"

Or let's say we go to church this Sunday and within five minutes of leaving the sanctuary we sin. What do we say to ourselves? "What a big hypocrite I am. I go sing religious songs and listen to a great sermon, but within five minutes of leaving, I blow it. Two steps forward, ten steps back... that's me." Or do we say to ourselves, "What I just did... that's the old way of acting. Wait a minute. That is *not* me; that's the old habits trying to reassert themselves. No way!"

THE HEALING POWER OF LOVE

There is a world of difference between those two responses. The first response believes that Jesus died and rose again but says, "If He did, He did it alone." The other response says, "No, I have died and have been raised to life with Him. What I did just then was not a reflection of who I most deeply am now as God's child."

When we truly understand and embrace the truth that God has made us into new people, we will live like who we believe we are. We will understand that when we sin, we are violating who we really are—what we've become as God's child. This means there are not two natures dwelling in us as God's children. When we came to Christ the old nature died, Christ came to dwell in us by His Spirit, and we were born again.

Our identity is the chief point of attack for the enemy—and if he can confuse us about who we are, he has won. That is why Paul says throughout his letters, "Don't you know who you are? You wouldn't do this if you really knew who you were." Paul instructs us to remind ourselves daily of who we have become.

As we allow the gospel in all its transforming power to penetrate us, we will be delivered from focusing on our problems and instead will focus on what God has accomplished for us through Christ.

At Home in the Family of the King

It is one of my core beliefs that who you *are* determines what you *do*. As someone once said, "Our actions are nothing more than belated announcements of our thoughts." So if you think of yourself primarily as a forgiven *sinner* (that means you see yourself as a sinner), then most likely you will continue to sin and beg forgiveness for it. But if you think of yourself as you truly are—pardoned, regenerated, and now a member of God's own family—your actions will quickly follow suit.

Let me ask: How do you think of yourself? As God's child? Because that's who you are! You are royalty—even though you may not always *feel* like it. Paul said it so well:

- ✦ You did not receive a spirit that makes you a slave again to fear, but you received the Spirit of sonship. And by him we cry, 'Abba, Father.' The Spirit himself testifies with our spirit that we are God's children. Now if we are children, then we are heirs—heirs of God and co-heirs with Christ (Romans 8:15-17a).

- ✦ Be imitators of God, therefore, as dearly loved children, and live a life of love, just as Christ loved us and gave himself up for us as a fragrant offering and sacrifice to God (Ephesians 5:1-2).

The glorious gospel truth is that you are a member of God's forever family. You are not a mistake or an embarrassment or anything else the devil wants you to believe that you are.

Peter Lord tells a great parable about a couple of young eaglets who fall from their lofty nest and are raised by turkeys. They grow up thinking they belong to the turkey crowd, but neither one can ever get too excited over the turkey kinds of things. "It is hard to be a turkey when you are an eagle," Lord writes. Then he describes the sad plight of one of these eaglets who was halfheartedly engaged in a hunt for acorns.

> He looked like most Christians I know—like he had been run over. He was dragging behind the crowd and he stopped under a tree. His head was down, his wings were dropped and he was saying, "O Lord, another day."
>
> There was an owl sitting up in the tree and that old owl looked down from his limb and saw that bedraggled-looking eaglet down there—defeated and discouraged. The owl asked, "Who-o-o-o are you? And what's wrong?" The eaglet answered, "I'm a turkey that's failing. I have tried so hard, but I can't make it. I don't even want to finish another day." The owl said, "Your problem is you don't know who-o-o you are. You're an eagle. Eagles are meant to be up there in the sky. You will never be happy down there on the ground in the dark woods."[7]

Lord's point is clear: We are eagles, not turkeys, and our dominion is the sky. I agree with Peter—I am thrilled to know I am an eagle! Aren't you? Or have you failed to grasp this tremendous reality? Get rid of "turkey theology"! Accept the truth that you are a beloved child of the Almighty God and that you share His nature and are a co-heir with Christ to all that God has. Don't keep telling yourself you are a turkey. "If you keep telling people they are turkeys," Lord writes, "they are going to keep acting like turkeys."[8] An eagle will act like a turkey until he discovers he is an eagle.

Why is it that so many of us have such a hard time accepting this truth about ourselves? Why do we struggle so much with accepting God's word to us about who He has made us to be? Just think of the spectacular panoramas that stretch out before us when we believe and act on God's assurances that we are, in fact, His children. I love the illustration Lord uses to emphasize this:

> Last Christmas I gave the gift that is easy to exchange to all my five children, three of whom are married. I gave them all money. I have a new daughter-in-law who kept saying to me, "You can't do this for us, you mustn't do this for us; it is too much . . . too much . . . too much." Do you know why she kept saying that? She did not know who she was because of her marriage to my son. My son said, "Daddy, keep it coming." None of those who *knew* they were my kids said, "You're doing too much for us." They just took it, and held out the other hand in case there was some more. But my daughter-in-law had not discovered who she was in my family. She has a new relationship and a new identity. She is my daughter, but she did not think of herself like that. She is the one who hurts because she did not know who she was. When we really know who we really are, we will have confidence with our Father.[9]

Then Lord asks,

Are you ready to reach out and say, "Lord, since you have given me the gift of right- eousness, then I am as righteous as you are. I receive it and am going to declare on the basis of what you have given me and what you have said, that this is true"? When this is written on our hearts, because we have re- ceived what God has given, it will begin to transform our lives in ways that we have never imagined. We will not be driven by the fear of failure. We will begin to live like who we are—sons and daughters of God; new cre- ations; saints; sanctified in Christ Jesus, full of all the grace that God has given us."[10]

Talk about the healing power of love! God loved us so much that He went to the extreme of sacrificing His own willing Son so He could win our healing. Through sin, all of us were wounded to the point of death—yet "how much more will those who receive God's abun- dant provision of grace and of the gift of righteousness reign in life through the one man, Jesus Christ" (Ro- mans 5:17).

It's true! God has done everything necessary for us to "reign in life." He left nothing undone. Nothing! But the choice is still ours, whether we will enjoy His provision. Will we enter into all the riches that God has provided for us? Will we choose to believe and ac- cept and *embrace* the healing power of love?

Will you? Why don't you pause right now and pray

out your acceptance of your healing, your transformation by God's love? Sure, it is a process, but it is also a gift. Take hold of it!

Where Are You Headed?

I heard about a fellow who was visiting cemeteries around the United States and reading the inscriptions on the tombstones in an attempt to find out more about his family roots. On one tombstone he found these words:

Pause now, stranger, as you pass by
as you are now, so once was I.
As I am now, so soon you'll be
so prepare yourself to follow me.

Standing next to the tombstone was a rough piece of wood and on it was scratched these words:

To follow you, I'm not content
until I know which way you went.

May I ask you a personal question? Which way are *you* headed? It is not enough to know *about* the life-changing truths we've been exploring in this chapter; they are part of us, infused in our hearts, ours to live out in our experience. God has fully equipped us to live as citizens of heaven even while we're down here on earth.

At the same time, however, I know that it is not easy to break away from long years of attachment to flesh patterns—the old ways of thinking are habit-forming.

Bad habits are deeply rooted in our mental processes. Some of these patterns of thinking, feeling, believing, and responding seem to flow out of us just as naturally as fruit grows on a tree. But they are lies—crab-apple "suckers" trying to take over our lives.

So even though we have been changed inwardly, changing our outward behavior often requires time, help from others, study in God's Word, and other gracious provisions of God's Spirit. In other words, changing our outward behavior to match the inward reality is very often a *process*. God understands that and He is eager to help us in that process.

But should this be such a big surprise? After all, He is the source and the dispenser of the healing power of love—and He'll see us all the way through to the end.

He promised!

8

A Moment to Be Cured, A Lifetime to Be Healed

*E*ven though I don't have a "big pain" problem,
I do struggle regularly with lower back pain. I'm
six-and-a-half feet tall, so getting in and out of cars, be-
ing forced to bend my back in the wrong way, and hav-
ing to stretch awkwardly has contributed to the problem.
Through an athletic injury—I have played basketball
for years—a disc in my back tends to pinch a nerve. When
that happens, the muscles in the right side of my back
tighten up. I went to see the doctor about it and after
taking a battery of X-rays he told me, "No, you definitely
don't want surgery. My recommendation is that you walk
a lot, which will help lubricate the disc. That should re-
lax your muscles and ease the pain."

To deal with my pain, then, I have to do something
regularly and continually. There was no one-time answer where the doctor could say, "Healed!" (Don't get
me wrong; it would be nice to have that.) But I have
discovered my healing is a process; it involves me. I

have to be careful. I may have a 21-year-old's desire to play basketball, but I'm living in a 49-year-old body. There are certain things I can no longer do.

If I follow the doctor's instructions and I'm careful, my back doesn't hurt. But when I neglect his advice and don't take care of my back, the pain returns.

So it is with the healing of our emotions. Many of the emotional wounds, disappointments, griefs, and hurts that we suffer can only be healed over time, sometimes a lifetime.

Living Out Our Healing

In the last chapter we emphasized that God's acceptance of us is not based on what other people think of us, what we've done in the past, or even what we think of ourselves now. Rather, His acceptance is based on His love for us and His gift of acceptance and restoration to friendship and adoption through the indwelling Holy Spirit.

But after we come to understand what God has done for us and we accept His wonderful gift, we must make the further admission that we may still have deeply ingrained habits of behavior that are in conflict with the fact that we are loved and accepted by Jesus Christ. That conflict creates a turmoil that necessitates a *process* of healing.

This year at our training institute in Colorado I led our students through the truth of justification by faith as it relates to sinful flesh patterns that dominate our lives. We enjoyed some sessions of teaching where real revelation was going on—students were weeping with joy, going to their rooms, coming back and saying, "I've got it! I understand now! It is hitting me; there's nothing I can *ever* do to make myself more loved. He just loves me!" It was tremendous. They were really grasping it, the depths of God's love!

But then as we got away from the emotional moment, the old patterns came back up. The old ways of dealing with problems returned. I began to say, "Hey, now we're talking about sanctification; we're talking about a *process* of healing as well as a *moment* of healing."

Emotional and spiritual healing is much like physical healing. Suppose you go to the doctor with a broken arm accompanied by a large gash. The doctor sees that your arm is broken and you have a huge cut. So he sets the bone, cleans the wound, stitches it up, and says, "Come back in two days." When you return, he sees some infection in the wound, so he reopens it and cleans it out. He's doing what is necessary for the process of healing to take place.

When I was 11 years old I was mowing the lawn for my dad. The lawnmower hit a stump, and because I wasn't paying attention, I ended up getting my foot—shod only in a flimsy tennis shoe—right under the lawnmower. The blade cut right through my shoe, stopped the motor, and left me with a huge gash on my foot. My dad heard my frantic howls for help, ran outside, loaded me in the car, and zipped me off to the hospital.

The doctor cleaned out the wound, gave me some shots, and sewed me up. Then he said the strangest thing. I thought we were done, but he said, "I want you to come back tomorrow."

The next day we obediently returned, and he did something that I thought was mean and nasty. He peeled off the bandage, looked at the wound, and said, "Ah-ha!"—which to an 11-year-old boy sounded especially ominous. He finished unwrapping the bandages, reopened the wound, and drew out some infection. Then he closed everything back up, smiled, and said, "Now it will be better."

I have since learned an important principle: When you're wounded emotionally, you have to keep that wound clean from bitterness, anger, revenge, hatred, and spite. This is a process; you can't clean the wound just once. Just like me and my foot injury, you're still sensitive . . . you're still hurting. Whenever you think of the person you associate with that hurt, there is a tendency to once again entertain negative thoughts about that person. That's the moment you have to clean the wound again.

We have *been* healed, so to speak, in that we have gone to the Great Physician; but we still have to work out the *process* of healing for the cure to be complete.

Seven Aspects of the Healing Process

What I'm about to share isn't a canned approach to the process of healing, although the subtitle, "Seven Aspects of the Healing Process," might sound like it. These are principles I have learned the hard way. I have hammered them out over 30 years of applying the great truths of who we are in Christ. These seven aspects are all crucial to our healing, but it's not as if you go through each one once and then the process is finished.

All of them are necessary all the way through the process; that's why I've called them "aspects" rather than "steps." Steps are taken one after the other. You leave one step behind you when you take the next step. In contrast, every one of these aspects is essential during the whole process.

1. *Be honest*

We can receive and experience God's healing love only to the degree that we are aware how much we need it and are consciously receiving it. If we deny that we have a problem and ignore it, we will fail to receive what God wants to give us to help us through our problem. We must be real about what has happened to us or how we're handling the difficult situations we face. If we're not honest, we won't be able to seek God's solution for us specifically or consciously.

Furthermore, if we are only superficially aware of our problem or pain, we may end up seeking only superficial remedies. Many of these superficial treatments are being offered both inside and outside the church. It is possible to take an aspirin for cancer or slap a Band-Aid on a festering sore, but these methods will always fail. Likewise, when it comes to dealing with our pain, we have to seek out God's solution.

Only when we are completely honest can we become truly spiritual. Spirituality is not just feeling good about ourselves and God; it's being honest and real with God. Then we can receive truth and grace from Him and appropriate His provisions to our area of need.

My wife and I strive to relate to each other honestly. We're open with each other no matter whether we're hurt or angry. Sally is absolutely unintimidated by me. I've written 11 books and have been on television all over the world, but when my little Texas wife doesn't like something I've done or said, she doesn't stop and say, "I'm sorry to bother you, dear Sir Floyd, great evangelist, but..." She just looks at me in the eye and says, "I don't want this, I don't take this; and don't talk to me like that!" My wife is *honest!*

God invites us to be honest with Him. He encourages us to be just as honest with Him as Sally is with me. He has invited us to be intimate with Him, and honesty is a big part of intimacy. It is crucial to be honest so that real healing can take place.

Honesty about my back pain is a key to taking care of it. There are times when I try to ignore my back pain because I think I've got to keep on going. But when my muscles tighten up, I tend to lean in one direction. Soon it becomes obvious to everybody that there's something wrong with me because I walk crooked. That usually happens to me once or twice a year.

Sometimes when my back is hurting and I'm standing there like the Leaning Tower of Pisa, people have asked me, "How are you doing?" "Fine," I've replied. "Well, you don't look fine," they say. "You're leaning!" So I admit, "Oh yeah. Well, my back hurts." I would try so hard to get my mind off my back pain that I wouldn't acknowledge it.

You know, we can do the same with emotional pain, disappointments, hurts, or fears. But God wants us to be ruthlessly honest with Him. We must be honest about what may be obvious to everyone but ourselves.

May I suggest that you take a moment right now to pray a simple prayer and commit yourself to living honestly before God? In fact, after each of the seven aspects I'm about to discuss, I'd like you to stop and commit yourself in prayer to the Lord.

Perhaps you could pray in this way:

> Lord, help me to be honest about my emotions and flesh patterns. When I react to somebody in anger, help me to acknowledge my anger. When I'm curt with my spouse or children or a friend, help me be honest, Lord. When I'm tired or feel discouraged, help me to be honest with myself—and You. Help me, Lord, to see the truth, to acknowledge it, and to act on that basis. In the name of Your Son Jesus I pray, Amen.

2. *Die daily to sin*

Sometimes sin is a willful choice on our part; more often, it is an unplanned reaction. We might react out of disappointment in a relationship, so we cut the person off. Maybe we respond critically because we feel hurt or betrayed. Or we might respond in unbelief; perhaps we are afraid of how people might hurt us if they get close to us, so we don't trust them or God. Whether our sin comes as an unplanned reaction or a deliberate choice, we are responsible to deal with it. But be careful here. God does *not* want you to repent of the emotional pain that occasioned the sin; you can't repent of being hurt. But we must take responsibility for our sinful *reactions* that spring out of hurtful feelings or circumstances. Thankfully, God has provided a way for us to do this.

When we sin, we need to remember our sin is not a reflection of who we are. If we have come to Christ in faith—with nothing in our hands but our need—and have placed our trust in Him for salvation, then we can rest assured that we are God's children and that His Spirit dwells within us. We are not two-natured people with an evil side and a spiritual side. Our old self was crucified with Him and He has created a new nature within us. Therefore, when we sin, that's not our identity. That's not who we are. That's not our nature any longer. Rather, we are children of God who have slid back into some old patterns.

Once we understand that, what are we to do? Paul declares three great truths in Romans 6 on which we are to take our stand:

   ` a. We have died to sin (verses 1-7);

   b. We know we are alive to Christ (verses 8-10);

   c. We are to yield ourselves to Christ (verses 11-14).

Building on that theology, I often pray something like this:

> Lord, I come to You because of what You've done for me on the cross. I thank You that when I accepted You into my heart, I died to my old way of living. Thank You that You've

come into my heart by Your Holy Spirit and You've forgiven me. But Lord, right now I'm hurt. [Or mad, disappointed, or... Try to be honest about the emotion you are feeling.] Lord, I turn away from temptation to sin. I'm sorry that I've even considered it. I don't want it. I thank You, Lord, that I have died with Christ on the cross to this sin and I consider myself to be dead to that sin from this moment on. And I receive by faith your provision through Your Holy Spirit because of Your death on the cross. I don't have to be a victim or a prisoner of sin. I am free through the resurrection power of Christ. Thank You, Jesus.

Note briefly the elements of this simple prayer: 1) Why I come (His death on the cross); 2) coming honestly; 3) coming in faith; 4) making a choice; and 5) receiving the blessing of that choice by faith. Then I thank the Lord for His help from that moment on. I pray in faith, in response to what He's done on the cross, and trust His promise that I am free. This doesn't mean I won't face another temptation or that the negative emotion will never arise again; but I can walk in the victory He already has won. How? Moment by moment I know I am dead to sin because I died with Christ on the cross.

3. *Appropriate God's healing love on a daily basis*

Upon the death of their wealthy father many years ago, two eccentric brothers from New York inherited a mansion and a lot of money. The brothers lived in the mansion, but fear drove them to board up every entrance to the house. They came and left their home only at night, and only through a second-floor window they had left unboarded. They never withdrew any of the money they had in the bank, but instead scoured the local dumps for usable trash.

Years went by. Finally the smell around their mansion got so bad that neighbors called the police. No one knew if anyone lived there. The police tried to enter the house through the front door but couldn't. Eventually they found the open second-floor window, crawled through it, and found the house filled with 60-some tons of trash.

One of the brothers was found dead in a steel trap he had built to keep out intruders. His corpse had been rotting for months. The other brother was found dead in a bed upstairs.

The brothers were rich, they had everything they needed, yet they refused to receive it and so lived off the garbage heap.

There are a lot of garbage-heap solutions offered to us these days. But don't live off them! Don't run from revival meeting to conference to counselor, looking for people to give you what God already has provided for you. *Receive what is yours.*

Everything we need is in Christ, and Christ is in us. Our healing is not a matter of trying to do something or to become something. We already are who He has made us to be. Our job now is to appropriate and receive who we are as sons and daughters of God with the power of the Almighty living in us.

Peter Lord tells a story about a woman who came into the receptionist's office at his church in Titusville, Florida.[1] The woman, a widow with children, was distraught because she had just received a speeding ticket that she could ill afford to pay. Peter wanted to cover part of the fine for her, but she didn't want to receive his gift. It took all his powers of persuasion to get her to take the money.

Lord then writes,

> I tried the same thing later with a little girl who came into the office. I said, "Honey, God has told me to give you ten dollars." She said, "Thank you."
>
> So what do you say to God when He tells you, "I accept you, I forgive you?" You say, "Thank you!" The little girl took it just that simply. That is what the Bible means when it says, "Whoever does not receive the kingdom of God like a child shall not enter it at all." It's our pride which keeps us from receiving what God wants to give us. Can you reach out to God and simply accept the abundance of grace and the gift of righteousness?[2]

Lord says this incident prompted him to ask God to turn him into a "professional receiver." What an interesting title! When I read that I began to wonder, *What is an amateur receiver?* An amateur receiver is not very skilled; he's part-time. But a professional is full-time and he's good at it. I'm with Peter Lord; I want to be a professional receiver!

How do we do that on a practical basis? When I'm struggling with a situation that I find overwhelming, I pray, "God, here's the situation. I need help. I refuse by Your grace to handle this the wrong way. But Lord, I can't do it myself. Will You now give me the grace, the strength, and the power of the Holy Spirit to respond the way You want me to? I receive and apply and appropriate Your grace and Your power right now to this situation. And I receive this by faith."

I do it just that simply. And so can you. If you're facing a difficulty right now, why don't you stop for a moment and pray a similar prayer?

The King of the Universe has not compromised His greatness. Rather, He has stepped down to our level and said, "I welcome you to receive all that I have. Everything I own is yours." Just as the father of the prodigal offered the elder brother everything he had, so also does God say to you now, "Everything I have is yours. Come and join the party!"

4. *Encourage relationships*

One weakness of some books that tackle the issue we're dealing with in *The Healing Power of Love* is that they're almost humanistic. That is, they seem to teach that if you just grasp the ideas in the book, everything will be great. They seem to imply that education is the answer to everything. But that's not true and it's not the way God intends for us to handle our problems and pain.

Truth is an indispensable foundation for health, but if you lack loving relationships (which the truth insists we have), you're not going to get healed.

Recently I've been going through an intense struggle in a relationship. I'm still working it out. Two friends have called me regularly and asked, "Floyd, how are you doing? How are you responding?" They've helped me walk through two big issues. They've encouraged me to be honest with myself to the Lord about how I'm feeling. And they've held me accountable to respond righteously.

I wouldn't have endured through my struggle without my friends Dave and Lynn. They've been a tremendous encouragement and a challenge to me. They have been channels of the grace and truth of Jesus into my life. They are not the source, but they have been active channels of God working in my life.

Seldom as individuals do we have the objectivity we require. We need loyal, loving, gracious friends who will both hold us accountable and encourage us. At times, my two friends have merely listened to me and encouraged me; at other times they've jumped all over me. But I know they're loyal to me, so I've taken it from them when they've been firm. That's what we need from our friends, and that's the kind of friend we need to be in return. At times, we lack the courage to be honest with people that we are close to. But when we fail to stand up to our friends and give them the kind of feedback they need to hear, we're actually letting them down. We can't afford that, and neither can they.

5. *Think the truth*

There are basically three ways you can get yourself messed up:

a. Think things that God doesn't say or believe about you;

b. Think things the devil does say about you;

c. Think false things other people have said about you.

Any one of these options is a sure recipe for defeat. The Bible says, "As [a man] thinketh in his heart, so is he" (Proverbs 23:7 KJV). To prove the point, I want to give you a guaranteed way to feel bad: Sit down and write out every failure in your life, every negative statement people have made about you, every lie that the enemy has spoken to you, and meditate on them all day. I promise you that you'll have a very, very bad day!

On the other hand, there is a direct link between meditating on God's promises, His declarations to us, His provision for us, and how He has worked through us. "Thank God, I'm not as sinful every day as I potentially could be!" Dr. Frances Schaeffer used to say. That's good to remember. Not everybody is as sinful as they could be. Christian, you're created in the image of God—so don't get sucked into worm theology; don't grovel and keep confessing how bad you are. Let's be more Christ-centered, not man-centered. Remember that Christ has made us into a new people.

Let's think the truth about ourselves!

It's like the car pulling the trailer. Where the car goes, the trailer goes. As we think the truth and choose the truth, our emotions are designed by God to follow and reinforce the truth. Or it's like the big chunk of vanilla ice cream on hot apple pie. The frozen confection provides an added incentive to eat the pie, but it's not the pie itself. Here's another way of looking at it: What would happen if you took a car and trailer out to the nearest freeway and started going backwards at 80 miles per hour? It wouldn't take long for you to have a wreck. Why? Because you're not using the car and trailer in the way they were designed.

In the same way, God never intended for emotions to lead us; He didn't design us to live by our feelings. That's why we must think the truth.

6. Live by truth, not by feelings

It's not enough to think the truth; we have to live it out.

Last year I counseled a bright, open young lady who had a bad habit of living by her feelings. When people hurt her, she got back at them because she felt like it. When she got tired, she'd disappear for days; after all, she felt like it. I tried to get her to see that the reason she struggled to think the truth about herself was that she had been allowing her emotions to rule her life.

This young woman *knew* the truth and at times she would tell herself the truth, but she habitually allowed her emotions to rule her. "Don't live by feelings," I challenged her, "live by the truth. Be honest with your feelings, lay them out before the Lord, but then choose righteousness. Build habits of righteousness, of goodness, of courtesy." Invariably she'd reply, "But I don't feel like it."

"That's okay," I'd say. "Don't feel like it. Be honest about that. But choose righteousness anyway."

"But that would make me a hypocrite," she'd protest.

"No, you're just fighting against negative emotions and you must decide that you won't let them rule you," I would insist.

I know firsthand this isn't always easy. I am a cross between a task-oriented visionary and a people-person. I love being around people and encouraging them, and I also like to dream big dreams.

Now, the task-oriented visionary in me loves a challenge and likes to believe God for great things, but he is not very emotional. Determined, yes, but not emotional. I see the task and I go for it. But the people side of me makes me susceptible to mood swings. It used to be that my emotions would determine how I would look upon a day. If I woke up and thought about a negative remark that had been thrown my way the day before, my whole day would be ruined, or at least a good part of it.

Eventually I came to understand that God made me to be sensitive to people. I *like* people. I like encouraging them. But because I'm sensitive, my emotions also swing back and forth. I can't let them rule me, so now I've learned to say, "Lord, I feel hurt. I'm upset. I'm angry [or whatever the emotion is] and I commit it to you. Help me to get on with life." I have found this helps my emotions to settle down.

Whether your emotions run a steady course or they swing wildly, God wants to empower you to live a consistent, godly life. And the way to do that is by *living out* the truth, not merely thinking it.

7. *Time*

It takes time to get over some things. We can't rush through wounds. Dr. Bob Pierce, the founder of World Vision, used to say to Sally and me, "Ninety percent of success is finishing." A lot of people quit along the way. Those who endure, those who hang in there, win. If there are ten runners in a race and nine drop out, the tenth runner wins, even if he's the slowest contestant on the track.

I like to say that the only failure in life is the failure to learn from our mistakes. In other words, experience is not the best teacher; *evaluated* experience is. As we go through life, there will be difficult lessons. Learning from them and growing through them takes time.

When I'm going through a hard time, I've learned *not* to ask, "Why is this happening to me, Lord?" When I approach it that way, I end up accusing God. On the other hand, I learn a lot when I say to God, "What do You want to teach me from this?"

It's plain from God's Word that He allows His children to be tested. He even arranges circumstances, events, or people in our lives to put us through a particular experience so He can teach us a specific lesson.

If we don't learn from our difficult or trying experiences, then we fail the test.

Let's consider the children of Israel in the wilderness. It was not God's plan for them to spend 40 years in the desert; He was disappointed that they didn't learn their lessons. Do you remember when God sent a dozen spies into the Promised Land? Ten of the men came back with a negative report, while the other two (Joshua and Caleb) returned with a positive one. Joshua and Caleb saw giants just as the other men did—they were honest—but they also believed God was greater than the giants. They learned the lesson while the others didn't. Because the other ten men were overwhelmed by what they saw, their circumstances became their god ... and they wound up licking dust in the desert until all of them were dead.

Sally and I lived in Amsterdam for 18 years. The last seven years there, Sally went through a hard time physically. One time my son Matthew and I returned from a mission trip to the Amazon, where we had visited church-planting teams working among tribal groups. Upon my return, Sally and I spent a couple of days just catching up with each other. "The pain has never been greater," she told me. This shocked me. My wife is not a complainer; she has a high pain threshold. "Some days," she admitted, "I just don't want to go on living."

I could hardly believe it. For years I had said, "We need to get you to a dryer climate; we need to get you to a better living situation." However, she had always said no. But when I said, "This time, maybe we need to move back to the States and get you some medical care and live in a warmer, dryer climate," she replied, "Well, maybe we should."

I was stunned. All of a sudden, I didn't feel like a great hero; I felt threatened. The main reason I made the offer was to play the role of a good husband—to be sensitive and loving. But when she took me up on the offer, I got nervous. I thought, *What if we really do leave Amsterdam? What will I do? Where will I go?* My whole identity was wrapped up in being an urban missionary who reached the inner city of Amsterdam.

As the months went by, I began to learn a lesson. A friend called me on the phone and said, "Floyd, I've been praying for you. You're not coming back to the States because Sally is sick. God is using Sally's health to redirect your life. He has something new for you." That word became a ray of light for me. I began to see a lesson I had learned before but now was learning in a new way: *God really is greater than our circumstances.* I could see Him using our difficult circumstances to redirect our lives.

It so happens that Sally's health has greatly improved since we returned home. But whether it improved or not, God had used our circumstances to create a whole new plan for our lives—to give us a new direction. (By the way, we are both really glad we followed God's new direction. We live in the beautiful Rocky Mountains of Colorado, where we oversee Mission Village. Write to us at P.O. Box 5, Trinidad, Colorado 81082, and we will send you information about what we do!)

Go to God in your difficult situations. Ask Him what He wants to teach you. Learn that lesson, let it become a part of your heart and life, and then build on it. If you're facing a hard circumstance, look to God. He can create something new for you. He did it for us, and He can take your bad situations, redeem them, and make them a blessing in your life. But remember this: It may take time. God never has been interested in shortcuts.

Take to the Heights

In the early days of aviation there was a pioneer flyer named Handley Paige.[3] Paige often flew to India. During one of his long flights he landed in a meadow. After resting awhile, Paige returned to his plane and took off. He had been in the air only a short time when he heard a gnawing sound behind him. He realized instantly what had happened. While on the ground, a rat had boarded his plane.

Paige fearfully listened as the rat gnawed away on some important wires right behind his head. He feared the rat would disable his craft and send it plummeting to the earth. In a panic, Paige suddenly recalled that rats can live only at low altitudes. Immediately he raised the plane's nose to the sun and flew as high as he and his craft could withstand. The air was so thin he could hardly breathe. He stayed at that altitude for the duration of his flight. When he landed, he looked behind him and found the rat. It was dead, suffocated by the heights.

When we are working through the emotional pains of our life, it is important for us to remember to fly high and stay close to God. He has already accomplished for us what we need to receive our healing. If we'll stay with the process He has ordained and fly as high as we can, He'll take care of the rest. So keep your eyes on Him, and He will deal with the rats!

9

BREAKING
THE POWER OF
SATAN'S LIES

---

*"*G*iuseppe Good-for-nothing"—that was the degrading name a San Francisco fisherman gave to his son. What disgusted him so was that the boy got sick at the mere smell of fish and turned green whenever he so much as saw a fishing boat. It didn't seem to matter that all his brothers loved the fishing business; Giuseppe hated it and didn't fit in. He tried to explain to his father that he could work in the office or in sales or in repairing the nets, but his father wouldn't listen. He insisted that his son either get on the boat or he would be "Giuseppe Good-for-nothing."*[1]

But Giuseppe couldn't get on the boat, so one day his father kicked him out of the business. "Get lost," he told him.

Giuseppe, of course, was devastated by this. He tried a few odd jobs, delivered newspapers, shined shoes, worked as a busboy in a restaurant. Every dime he made he gave to the family, but since he wasn't fishing, his father kept calling him "Giuseppe Good-for-nothing."

When Giuseppe didn't feel accepted or loved at home, he started hanging out in the streets. There he discovered a sport called stickball. Giuseppe was *good*. Blessed with lightning hands and fleet feet, he could hit, run, and field the ball with the best of them. As a result, an impossible dream began to take shape in his heart.

Out of the rejection and the cruel accusations flung at him by his father, Giuseppe began to discover for himself the truth about who he was. He followed his dream, persevered, and by the time he achieved it, Giuseppe had become one of the most successful members of his family. He even convinced two of his brothers to quit the fishing business and follow him.

After many years, a day arrived when Giuseppe's father wept with pride at the accomplishments of his "good-for-nothing" son. Giuseppe was reconciled to his father through his refusal to believe the lie.

Years later, long after his career had ended, Giuseppe would lovingly laugh and recall his pain the day his father kicked him off the boat. He said it was the best thing that ever happened to him—for you see, Giuseppe not only persevered after being ejected from the family business, but he went on to earn the nickname "Joltin'" Joe DiMaggio, a larger-than-life member of professional baseball's Hall of Fame.

Fighting the Enemy's Lies

Every day and from many directions, false accusations are constantly being hurled against us. Some of them are spoken unintentionally by family members; some are cruelly thrown at us by children; others are used by the enemy himself to wound us like daggers piercing our heart.

Whether we like it or not, spiritual warfare plays a big part in receiving and keeping our healing. The devil does not want to see you whole. Our Lord said Satan was a liar and a murderer from the beginning, and many of his lies are aimed squarely at robbing us of the salvation and wholeness God has given us.

The apostle Paul wrote in 2 Corinthians 10:4 that "the weapons we fight with are not the weapons of the world. On the contrary, they have divine power to demolish strongholds." Throughout his two letters to the Corinthians, Paul was addressing problems in the church. He saw their problems not merely as personality disorders, emotional difficulties, or leadership conflicts, but rather as demonic attempts by Satan to attack God's people.

There's not a Christian alive who has failed to experience one of these attacks. Satan does all he can to hurt us by hurling lies against our minds. When we fail to use our spiritual resources to dislodge these thoughts and get rid of them, they take root in our minds and become entrenched there. The Bible calls them "strongholds" (2 Corinthians 10:4).

I've come to the conclusion that a stronghold is any lie we believe that keeps us from embracing the love and acceptance of Jesus. Some people believe all the right doctrine but never allow that truth to sink into their deepest personhood. They still *act* as if it weren't true even though they would pass Theology 101 with the highest honors. So what keeps them from living in the fullness of the truth that they believe? In many cases, it's a stronghold.

And spiritual warfare is the only way to get rid of it.

The story is told of a man who went to see a doctor. When the doctor diagnosed his problem, the man grew indignant. "I want a second opinion," he demanded. The doctor replied, "Okay; you're ugly, too."

Many Christians don't like it when they hear the truth because the truth demands personal responsibility. We learned in the previous chapter that healing is a process and that God wants to involve us in that process. He could do it all for us, but He doesn't. We have our part to play.

The same is true in fighting the lies of the enemy. The devil has millions of ways to deceive us, lie to us, or attack our minds, but there is only one way for us to be free from sin—through submitting our lives to the Lord Jesus and receiving His gift of life and grace and truth. We're not saved by information about the truth but by revelation born out of desperation, which leads to transformation.

Truth Is the Answer

Satan's power is in the lies he tells us. He does not work with truth; he works with deception. Jesus said Satan cannot hold to the truth, "for there is no truth in him. When he lies, he speaks his native language, for he is a liar and the father of lies" (John 8:44). Satan has no power over us except through the lies he speaks and we believe. His lies—about who we are or how we must behave or who God is—become the strongholds that keep us from the knowledge of Christ.

Since Satan's weapons against us are based on lies, our only defense against him is the truth. Neil Anderson says, "Dealing with Satan is not a power encounter; it's a truth encounter."[2] When we speak the truth against Satan, we expose his lie and gain power over him.

In one of His prayers to the Father, Jesus said, "My prayer is...that you protect them from the evil one. ...Sanctify them by the truth; your word is truth" (John 17:15,17). And Paul said the way to transformation is through the renewing of our minds (Romans 12:2).

This means we must do away with all fruitless fantasy and the vagrant thoughts that can never build us up in our faith. "Whatever is true, whatever is noble, whatever is right, whatever is pure, whatever is lovely, whatever is admirable—if anything is excellent or praiseworthy—think about such things," Paul instructs us in Philippians 4:8.

Further, it is not only possible but essential for us as Christians to "take captive every thought to make it obedient to Christ" (2 Corinthians 10:5). We must be aggressive in rejecting every thought that in any way could oppose the truth. Evaluate everything that comes into your mind by one simple test: Does it build you up in your faith? By doing this, you are inviting the Holy Spirit of God to rule in your thoughts and emotions. Then you can claim the promise of Philippians 4:7: "and the peace of God, which transcends all understanding, will guard your hearts and your minds in Christ Jesus."

In his book *The Search for Significance*, Robert McGee says:

> As an offensive weapon, repentance has two sharp edges. The first allows us to discern and reject false beliefs. When situations occur which trigger certain beliefs that produce ungodly responses, we must: 1) be honest about our emotions; 2) trace the emotions back to their source and identify the false beliefs; 3) consciously and assertively reject the false beliefs.[3]

This is why we battle against every lie and bring every thought into captivity. We must not allow any thought to take us captive, but rather we take them captive and submit them to the truth of who God is and what He says about us as His children.

Overcoming the pain in our lives means we enter a battlefield. We must be prepared to battle for the truth. The enemy will fight us with lies, and those who are not ready to engage in this kind of spiritual warfare will be overcome. Not every stronghold of the enemy goes away when we get saved. Some of them are left for us to destroy with the help of spiritual resources granted to us by a loving God.

What Is a Stronghold?

Let's try to define a stronghold a bit further. A

stronghold is any entrenched area in our experience where the devil has some foothold in controlling that part of our lives. It's an area of ingress where we have given Satan rights into our thoughts, whether through pain, weakness, sin, or bad theology. It's a place where untruth—a lie—rules our thoughts, where the devil has inroads to us because we believe his lie. It is an area where Satan has actively engaged us in battle—and is temporarily defeating us.

This area may have roots going back to childhood. It could include habits formed over the years. It could be a food disorder. It could be a problem in our family or a flesh pattern. A stronghold is anything that gives the devil a foothold on which to speak a convincing lie to us—anything in our character or emotions that serves as a platform on which he can stand to shout into our ear something untrue about ourselves or God.

Some of these lies have an *emotional* side to them. We may not believe them consciously, but somehow we have accepted as true certain things that are false, and they become a belief system for us. Emotional lies might include deep insecurity that remains unresolved, shame that's buried, guilt that's undealt with, or fear that has taken root in our heart without being confronted. All of these are emotional footholds that give the enemy a platform from which he can encourage us to believe a lie about how God sees us or who He is.

Let's say, for example, that we experienced rejection in our childhood. The enemy could say to us, "Who has ever *really* been committed to you unconditionally? There's no one." By saying this he seeks to undermine our trust in the Living God, not just in people. That is a stronghold.

Let's say you were abused. The enemy speaks the lie, "You can trust no one. Never put yourself in the presence of a man and trust him." His goal is not merely to undermine your trust in men generally, but specifically to cause you to doubt our Father who is in heaven. This too is a stronghold.

There are also *theological* lies that the enemy speaks against the character of God. "He is not really faithful," Satan whispers. "There are some things He just won't forgive." Or, "You have to do this, you have to do that. If you don't, He won't accept you." Sometimes our head understands these to be lies, but our heart fears that these lies are true.

Some of us might be tempted to question the work of Christ on the cross. "You aren't one of the elect," Satan lies. "You couldn't be! Look what you just did. No real Christian could ever do that." As we keep these fears to ourselves, they begin to gnaw away at our souls and before long, we're not sure God has forgiven us.

Sometimes a theological lie can find a resting place in our hearts through a disappointment. Perhaps we feel as though God promised us something but then let us down. This disappointment undermines our confidence in His promise to adopt us, give us a new identity, and forgive everything in our life. The enemy then uses this stronghold to sow further lies about God's character.

Then there are the *mental* lies that the enemy speaks directly to our mind, the ugly little statements or thoughts that seem to come from nowhere. "You can't trust spiritual leaders," he murmurs. "They are all like the TV evangelists. You can't submit to any spiritual authority—especially not God's. How can you trust Him? He's not here. Besides, He's never gone through what you've gone through." Or, "You're not good enough. You're dumb. You're not pretty enough; you're a failure. Why don't you just give up?"

A stronghold can be constructed in our minds—mentally or emotionally or theologically, one brick at a time—until a giant fortress is built up. It takes on a tremendous force and power of its own. It stands between us and the knowledge of Christ, as the Scripture says. This stronghold must be detected for what it is and then destroyed.

How to Detect a Stronghold

As a rule, the only way to detect a stronghold is to know the truth and compare that truth with what you see in your life. Most strongholds can be placed in one of three categories.

1. *A stronghold is anything contrary to what God's Word says about us.*

Anything that we believe about ourselves that contradicts Scripture is a lie. For example, homosexuality is a stronghold. A young lady once said to me, "I'm gay." She was a Christian who was struggling with past sin. Through her intense struggle, she had concluded that the only way she was going to have peace was to give in and accept homosexuality as her identity. I told her,

"That's not who you *are,* that's what you've *done."* God has created us male and female. Even if we don't *feel* male or female, that is still what we are by birth.

I don't think it's an accident that the book of Ephesians deals at length with the subject of spiritual warfare (Ephesians 6:10-18). Why is it no surprise? Because the first few chapters deal so powerfully with the revelation of who we are in Christ. In those chapters, Paul affirms repeatedly that our identity and security are to be found in Christ alone. Of course the enemy is going to attack that kind of truth! So God takes pains in chapter 6 to tell us of the spiritual warfare we can expect.

You can expect to battle against the lies of the enemy about your identity, your worth and your heritage. He wants to rob you of what's yours—or rather, trick you out of receiving it. But don't let him get away with it. Fight his lies with gospel truth!

2. *A stronghold is anything that speaks against God's character.*

I have a friend who went through a difficult time during his second year in seminary. He was under a lot of pressure and eventually his body reacted to the stress. Within a few weeks he was convinced that he was in serious medical trouble. At the same time, terrible thoughts about God started filling his mind. *What if God isn't really as good as He claims to be? What if He's really evil? What if He's getting a good laugh at your expense? Here you are, training to serve Him, and now He rewards you with illness? What if He's not kind or loving at all, but instead is an omnipotent devil?*

Have you ever had thoughts like that? Have you ever questioned God's goodness, love, or faithfulness? Have you ever thought that God might not be telling you the whole truth about His character . . . that there's a secret side to Him that He doesn't allow anyone to see—until it's too late?

If so, rest assured that you're not alone. That happens to all of us at one time or another. This is one of Satan's most common tactics: to question God's character. Remember, that was his whole strategy in the Garden of Eden: "Did God really say, 'You must not eat from any tree in the garden'? . . . You will not surely die . . . for God knows that when you eat of it your eyes will be opened, and you will be like God, knowing good and evil" (Genesis 3:1,4-5). Satan's strategy with Eve—and unfortunately for us, it worked—was to get her to doubt what God had said. That, in turn, would cause her to doubt His loving character.

If Satan can get us to believe his lies and doubt God's truth, then he has won. And we've lost. The only way to stand against these lies is to know the truth about God's character and refuse to budge from that truth even when circumstances might stir doubts in our mind. Satan got Eve to believe that God was a liar, and look where it got us. What if she had stood on the truth? What a different world it would be today!

3. A stronghold is any lie about what Christ has done for us to make us His son or daughter.

The devil loves to attack our confidence that Christ died for us. He doesn't mind if we believe that Jesus loves the world and died to redeem it—as long as he can get us to doubt that "the world" includes us.

I have counseled many people who struggled mightily with believing that Jesus could forgive them. They believed they were too dirty. Too sinful. Too wild. Too reckless. They had an abortion. They committed adultery. They had committed "the unpardonable sin." They had lost their salvation.

But the truth of the gospel still stands: "Here is a trustworthy saying that deserves full acceptance: Christ Jesus came into the world to save sinners—of whom I am the worst" (1 Timothy 1:15).

The Bible insists that "while we were still sinners, Christ died for us" (Romans 5:8). When the enemy starts questioning the fact that God loves us and Christ died for us, even in the midst of our sin, then we can know that he is trying to build up a stronghold in our mind. We must stand directly against him.

We can be certain that the enemy has established strongholds in our hearts and minds when we struggle emotionally to accept God's gift of grace and adoption. If we feel hostile toward the Lord; if there is unbelief in our heart; if there is rebellion against His authority; if there is mistrust of His Word; if there is hesitation about who He has made us to be; if we doubt His love, goodness, holiness, and trustworthiness; then we can be sure the enemy has been at work, speaking lies to our minds, seeking to establish strongholds in our lives. If we see in our character consistently wrong actions or rotten fruit, then we can know the root problem is a stronghold that has been established by the enemy.

How to Destroy a Stronghold

So how do we destroy strongholds? As in any war, we use weapons. And what are those weapons? Since this is a spiritual war, we need spiritual weapons. Those weapons include the Word of God; knowing and speaking His Word; the redeeming work of Christ on the cross; speaking the truth about God and His character; walking in the light about our weaknesses; worshiping God (especially in the midst of crisis); and resisting Satan and his lies through faith in God.

And how do we exercise these weapons? We must keep the following in mind:

1. *There must be a desperation that motivates us to cry out to God for help.*

This desperation is the difference between those who merely recognize a stronghold and those who pull it down. Desperation is urgency; it is a refusal to allow the stronghold to remain. It expresses itself through prayer, through resisting Satan (James 4:7) and his lies, and choosing truth, no matter what the cost.

Several times in my life, I have said to the Lord that I want to be a man of truth no matter what the cost. I have welcomed God and given Him an invitation to do whatever He wants to do so that I could be conformed to the image of His Son. I have been tested in this commitment many times, but I remain committed to being a man of truth.

2. *We need to ask God how the lie of the enemy achieved a foothold in our lives.*

What is the platform the enemy is using to whisper his untruths to us? What is the framework he has built that supports the surrounding lies? "Nobody loves you. Nobody cares for you. Nobody remembers your birthday." Ask God to show you all the little, nagging thoughts that eat away at your sense of importance, dignity, or worth. What triggers the lie to come to the surface in your mind? A feeling of fear, anger, guilt, or shame? Trace that feeling to its roots, and you can identify how the foothold got established.

3. *Turn from the lie.*

Once you know what the lie is, repent of believing it. Confess to the Lord Jesus that you have given in to that lie, and then believe in and speak the truth of what God says. This can be as simple as renouncing and turning from such lies as:

+ God can't use me. I'm a nobody.

+ I'm so ugly that I can't ever be attractive to anybody. How could I ever share the gospel with someone?

+ It must be my fault that my parents don't love each other.

+ My father was an alcoholic, so I'm bound to be an alcoholic as well.

+ My mother abandoned our family. I just know deep inside I'll do the same to my own family.

+ There has been a pattern of suicide in my family, one generation after another. It's bound to happen to me.

+ I know God speaks to other people and gives them direction and helps them, but I don't believe He can do that for me.

+ Other people can memorize Scripture, but I can't do it. I'm dumb. I'm a failure.

Turn from those lies and accept the truth of what God says about you. You are not trapped in a situation without hope unless you choose to be. Specifically think through the truth in response to each lie you have accepted from Satan, and stand on that truth each time the lie comes into your mind.

4. Receive God's love and acceptance.

Jesus is our inheritance. He is our friend, counselor, and Savior. He is our forgiver and the truth upon which we stand. Why don't you take a moment to meditate on just a few of the "I am" statements uttered by Christ in the Gospels? Commit to memory the statements Jesus made that apply to your life or situation. Remember, He is all of these things for us:

+ "I am gentle and humble in heart, and you will find rest for your souls" (Matthew 11:29).

+ "I am with you always, to the very end of the age" (Matthew 28:20).

✦ "I am among you as one who serves" (Luke 22:27).

✦ "I am the bread of life. He who comes to me will never go hungry, and he who believes in me will never be thirsty" (John 6:35).

✦ "I am the light of the world. Whoever follows me will never walk in darkness, but will have the light of life" (John 8:12).

✦ "I am not alone. I stand with the Father, who sent me" (John 8:16).

✦ "I am the gate; whoever enters through me will be saved. He will come in and go out, and find pasture" (John 10:9).

✦ "I am the good shepherd. The good shepherd lays down his life for the sheep" (John 10:11).

✦ "I am God's Son" (John 10:36).

✦ "I am the resurrection and the life. He who believes in me will live, even though he dies" (John 11:25).

✦ "I am the way and the truth and the life. No one comes to the Father except through me" (John 14:6).

✦ "I am in my Father, and you are in me, and I am in you" (John 14:20).

✦ "I am the vine; you are the branches. If a man remains in me and I in him, he will bear much fruit; apart from me you can do nothing" (John 15:5).

Jesus is holding out His arms toward you this very moment. He invites you to accept all that He is for you—to embrace it, live by it, and thrive in it. This isn't wishful thinking; it is the truth. And it is the only way to enjoy the emotional healing God longs for you to have.

Confronting Bad Habits

I've heard it said many times by new Christians, "Life has been much harder since I became a Christian." One reason life seems more difficult is that the old habits of gratification, once accepted and eagerly yielded to, are now being confronted by the Holy Spirit. You are now reading the Word, being exposed to Christian teaching, and realizing you have a responsibility to live in a way that pleases God. As a result, the old gratification mechanisms and habits are being confronted. It's only as those old ways are overcome and new habits of righteousness are built up that a person begins to see growth and maturity.

A long time ago I heard one Christian say something like this: "Sow a thought, reap a choice; sow a choice, reap a habit; sow a habit, reap a character; sow a character, reap a destiny."

It's amazing how quickly habits can be formed. I believe they can be formed in a matter of days, although some people say it takes as long as six weeks. Either way, that's not a long time. Exercising a bad habit long enough establishes a platform for the enemy to plant a lie in your mind.

I have an Australian friend named Rod whose parents took in a retarded cousin when Rod was still a young boy. This cousin had some severe handicaps and was verbally abusive toward my friend. When Rod's parents left him alone to take care of his abusive cousin, he got the thought in his mind that they didn't love him. To this day, anytime someone speaks strongly to Rod or looks at him harshly, it triggers the traumatic memory of being with that cousin and makes him susceptible to believing that he is not loved. Until Rod resolved that situation and forgave his parents and that cousin, he could not receive and appropriate the truth of God's love and acceptance for him and through him to others. It was a stronghold in his life.

Neil Anderson helps us to understand how this works by asking us to imagine three boys, ages 18, 13, and 9, whose father becomes an alcoholic. "When the father comes home drunk and belligerent every night, the oldest son is big enough to stand up for himself. He says to his father, 'You lay one hand on me, buster, and you're in trouble.' The middle child can't resist his dad physically, so he becomes the classic enabler, seeking to appease him. He greets his dad with, 'Hi Dad, are you feeling okay? Can I get you anything?' The youngest son is simply scared stiff of his father. When dad comes home, he scurries out of sight and hides in the closet or under the bed. He stays clear of his dad and avoids conflict."[4]

Anderson points out that the tendencies established in these three boys' lives later become platforms on which flesh patterns are established, which eventually turn into strongholds of the enemy. He writes, "As the three boys continue in their defensive reactions to their hostile, alcoholic father, they form patterns of behavior. Ten years later, when these young men face any kind of hostile behavior, how do you think they will respond? The oldest one will fight, the middle one will appease, and the youngest one will run away."[5]

Anderson is not saying that they *must* respond in those ways; he is saying they will encounter temptations that lead them to act in those ways. He then says, "That's the way they've learned to handle hostility. Their deeply ingrained patterns of thinking and responding have formed strongholds in their minds."[6]

Remember, a stronghold is any lie of the enemy about how you have to act, or anything you believe that keeps you from experiencing the reality and power of Christ. Hostility is a stronghold in the life of the oldest son; manipulation is a stronghold for the second son; and fear is a stronghold in the heart of the youngest son. If these strongholds are not identified, broken, and replaced with the truth of Christ, none of these boys will live in the complete emotional healing that God wants them to enjoy.

The Goal: Enjoying God

We were designed to live in fellowship with God to fulfill His purposes. As John Piper says, "The chief aim of man is to glorify God *by* enjoying Him forever."[7]

Yet from the day we were born, there have been relationships, circumstances, events, places we've been, and experiences we've suffered that send another message to us: namely, that God does not want us and that we cannot enjoy Him. We are influenced, however briefly, by books we read, movies we watch, music we listen to, and traumatic events that we experience. Many of them speak the lie to us that we cannot live in fellowship with God, we cannot enjoy Him forever, and we cannot fulfill His purposes for our life. We have even adapted our ways of living to avoid the pain these experiences bring us. We've built up ways of coping that substitute for dependence upon Jesus and His grace.

When we become Christians our sins are washed away, but God does not begin to control our mind and force us to think in godly ways. Though in reality He has made us His beloved children, sometimes we still aren't certain if our adoption into His family is genuine and 100 percent unconditional.

Our job, then, is to cooperate with the process in which our minds catch up with the reality of what has happened to us. As we learn to put our trust in the Lord, our emotions begin to line up with our thoughts. It's imperative for us to exercise our will in this process.

For example, if a man has a fight with his wife and he feels rejected, misunderstood, and bitter, there may be a great temptation for that man to lust. He could look at a pretty woman or at a suggestive photograph or movie and be more susceptible to lust than he would have been before the fight. He will have to be on his guard not to give in. One of the ways he can fight back is by exercising the spiritual weapon of truth. He can walk in the light with the Lord.

He can say right there to the Lord Jesus, "Lord, I am hurt by my wife, but I refuse to allow anything to come into my mind that suggests the only way I can find comfort in this situation is with another woman or through looking at pictures of women. I choose to believe the truth. I choose to rejoice in the wife You have given me. And I trust that You are going to bring healing and wholeness into our relationship."

In that way the man rejects the temptation and the lie that he needs to do something sinful to be comforted. As he does this, he is directly confronting old habits or ways of life. And he is winning the spiritual battle.

Take That Fortress!

Mary is a responsible university graduate. She was helping to run a large business but was working under an abusive supervisor. Her uncomfortable situation brought up a lot of painful memories from her past of how she had been mistreated by spiritual authority figures. Mary had started believing some of the things her supervisor said to her—that she was dishonest, insubordinate, and irresponsible. She began to lose objectivity and could not see where she had made mistakes at work, where those supposed mistakes ended, and where her true identity began.

Mary was in quite an emotional state when I met her. As I listened to her, I asked questions to try to grasp the circumstances and sense what God was doing in her life and how He might want to use her situation.

I soon concluded Mary was in denial about what her boss had done to her. She was nursing a lot of anger.

When I asked her, "What do you feel God is teaching you?" and "How do you feel you should respond?" I got a lot of excuses. I heard angry descriptions about how bad and unfair her boss was and how difficult the circumstance was. As this went on, I tried to keep affirming Mary. I genuinely empathized with her; it *did* seem very unfair.

But as I gently returned to my question, "What do you feel God wants you to do?" Mary started repeating the lies of the devil. "I can't do that. I've never been able to forgive. I've never been able to confront." I did not force the issue with her, but I did encourage Mary that with God's help, her emotions did not have to enslave her. Nor did the words of her boss have to determine how she felt about her character or destiny. I stressed that God had purposes for the situation that were greater than her circumstances, and that if she would obey God, He would enable her to overcome them.

Eventually there came a point in our counseling where Mary began to believe that God would help her. She identified the stronghold that had been keeping her in bondage, rejected it, and turned to God's truth about herself and her responses. She went back to her boss, faced him, and told him how she felt about the way he had treated her. Then she told him she forgave him.

This was a tremendously liberating experience for Mary as she faced her own feelings, faced the wrong choices and actions of her boss, and went on to forgive him. God was at work in her life, partnering with her to pull down the strongholds that kept her bound.

No stronghold of Satan can stand up to the truth. Though they all seem strong and impregnable in the darkness, they melt away like castles of cobweb in the bright light of the gospel of Christ. We are justified by faith, and that's where we must put our trust. We don't have to trust in being a successful businessman, a powerful pro athlete, or the life of the party. We *can* be those things, but we don't *have* to be those things to feel secure when we go home at night.

Our security is found in Christ alone. And He has posted signs on all His territories, "No Strongholds Allowed." We just have to make sure we don't take down the signs!

10

KISS THE
TALKING FROG

*C*haplain *David Brown was walking beside a line of Abram's tanks and M2 Bradley Fighting Vehicles when the message blared across the radio.*[1] *He and other members of his unit were in Iraq, poised to attack a Republican Guard division during Operation Desert Storm. The excited voice cried out, "Incoming! We have a man down."*

Brown immediately climbed into a tank turret not only to better hear the report but also to seek protection from what might be raining down upon him. Confusion reigned. Were they under attack?

Despite a jumbled torrent of voices and heavy static on the radio, the chaplain heard that a soldier nearby had been walking among some Iraqi bunkers when there had been an explosion. It looked as if the man had been caught in a minefield. Brown quickly jumped from the tank and ran through the minefield to get to the wounded soldier. When he arrived, other men were already loading the man onto a medic's vehicle. The soldier saw Brown's insignia and cried out, "Ride with me, sir, please!"

The chaplain climbed onto the vehicle and grimaced at what he saw—an exposed upper thigh and a bloody, mangled stump where the soldier's leg had been. Brown tried to comfort the man, prayed with him, and rode with him until they reached a helicopter pad, where the soldier was airlifted to a hospital. The chaplain then sat down and wept, wondering what more he could have done.

Weeks later Brown was invited to attend a dinner hosted by the company to which the wounded soldier belonged. The soldier was there, in a wheelchair, greeting his friends. Brown approached him anxiously, once again aware of a strong feeling of helplessness. Yet there was no need for anxiety. The soldier wheeled up to Brown and said, "Thanks for being there, chaplain. I needed your prayers. I could not have made it without you."

Yet all Brown had done was comply with a soldier's battlefield request to ride with him. That was all the man had wanted—somebody to be with him in the midst of his pain.

You know, that's really all that most of us want—somebody to be with us in the midst of our pain. It doesn't have to be on a battlefield and it doesn't matter whether you're a chaplain. People in pain just want *you,* your presence, your understanding.

The Danger of Looking Too Hard for Love

There is a danger in focusing *too much* on God's

healing love. We can become so focused on what God can do for us that we actually become "selfish on love." Yet a proper understanding of God's love will always lead us to focus on serving others. By its very nature, love is unselfish. It gives of itself. So if we truly understand and appropriate the healing power of God's love, we will want to share it with others. *God heals us so that we will go out into the world to be instruments of healing for others.*

There is nothing sadder than to be around a person whose entire focus is on what he can get from God for himself. "Save me, heal me, fill me, deliver me—so I can sit here and enjoy You forever." No! That's not what God's healing love is all about. We will know we are on the way to true, godly healing when we can't wait to tell others about what Christ is doing for us. When we see others through God's eyes. When we're willing and eager just to serve others without recognition.

It saddens me that the cult of self has such an enormous pull in our modern, affluent culture. Yes, it's wonderful to see all that God has done for us and to emphasize the importance of seeing people set free from their life-controlling habits. And yes, it's also helpful to see that we're not just sinners, but we're also sinned against. However, taking these truths to an extreme will cause us to become imbalanced, ingrown, and unhealthy.

In 1992 a Los Angeles County parking control officer came upon a brown Cadillac El Dorado illegally parked next to the curb on street sweeping day.[2] The officer dutifully wrote out a $30 ticket and placed it on the dashboard, completely ignoring the man seated behind the wheel of the car. Perhaps to the officer's surprise, the man in the car made no excuses, did not attempt to argue, and made no moves to refuse the ticket.

And for good reason: The man was dead! He had been shot in the head ten to twelve hours earlier but his body was still sitting up, stiff as a board, slumped slightly forward with blood on his face. The officer, preoccupied with his job, later said he was unaware of anything out of the ordinary. He got back in his car and drove off.

As gruesome as the story is, it points to an important truth for the church. Many people around us are dying in their sin and their pain, but we are oblivious to their plight. Instead of helping them, we're busy checking off their infractions and misdemeanors. While they're dying, we're writing out tickets for illegal parking.

Comforted to Comfort

Other than the Lord Jesus Himself, I doubt that anyone in the New Testament suffered as much or experienced as much pain as the apostle Paul. Even at his conversion the Lord said of him, "I will show him how much he must suffer for my name" (Acts 9:16).

While the book of Acts details those sufferings, in some ways Paul's own recollection of them is more telling. In two remarkable passages in 2 Corinthians, he gives an autobiographical report of the sufferings that fulfilled his Lord's prediction:

As servants of God we commend ourselves in every way: in great endurance; in troubles, hardships and distresses; in beatings, imprisonments and riots; in hard work, sleepless nights and hunger... through glory and dishonor, bad report and good report; genuine, yet regarded as impostors; known, yet regarded as unknown; dying, and yet we live on; beaten, and yet not killed; sorrowful, yet always rejoicing; poor, yet making many rich; having nothing, and yet possessing everything (2 Corinthians 6:4-10).

I have worked much harder, been in prison more frequently, been flogged more severely, and been exposed to death again and again. Five times I received from the Jews the forty lashes minus one. Three times I was beaten with rods, once I was stoned, three times I was shipwrecked, I spent a night and a day in the open sea, I have been constantly on the move. I have been in danger from rivers, in danger from bandits, in danger from my own countrymen, in danger from Gentiles; in danger in the city, in danger in the country, in danger at sea; and in danger from false brothers. I have labored and toiled and have often gone without sleep; I have known hunger and thirst and have often gone without food; I have been cold and naked. Besides everything else, I face daily the pressure of my concern for all the churches (2 Corinthians 11:23-28).

As if that weren't enough, just a chapter later the apostle tells us how a "messenger of Satan," a "thorn in the flesh," was sent to "torment" him (2 Corinthians 12:7). Three times he asked the Lord to remove this torment, but the Lord refused. The thorn would stay. So far as we know, Paul continued to suffer with this tormenting thorn until the day he died.

Now put this all together. Wouldn't you agree that the apostle knew a thing or two about suffering? That he could talk with experience and authority about what to do with pain?

Remember, this is the man who wrote, "I rejoice in what was suffered for you, and I fill up in my flesh what is still lacking in regard to Christ's afflictions, for the sake of his body, which is the church" (Colossians 1:24). This is the man who wrote, "It has been granted to you on behalf of Christ not only to believe on him, but also to suffer for him, since you are going through the same struggle you saw I had, and now hear that I still have" (Philippians 1:29-30).

Beyond all argument, Paul knew about suffering. He was intimately acquainted with pain. And that's why I think his words at the beginning of 2 Corinthians are so tremendously significant:

> Praise be to the God and Father of our Lord Jesus Christ, the Father of compassion and the God of all comfort, who comforts us in all our troubles, so that we can comfort those in any trouble with the comfort we ourselves have received from God. For just as the sufferings of Christ flow over into our lives, so

also through Christ our comfort overflows (2 Corinthians 1:3-5).

That is remarkable. The very letter in which the great apostle recounts his lifelong sufferings begins with the principle that God comforts us in our pain so that we can comfort others in pain.

Paul suffered in ways most of us can never imagine. He also had been comforted in his sufferings. But that was not enough for him. He wasn't content to be comforted. He realized that one of the primary reasons the Lord had comforted him was so that he, in turn, could seek out and comfort others who needed to experience the infinite compassion of Christ.

But how do we bring God's comfort to those in pain? How do we use God's response to our painful experiences as a springboard for ministry? I believe we have a simple, twofold responsibility in helping people through the healing process:

1. *Discern* what God is doing in their life;

2. Help them *cooperate* with God.

That's it, in a nutshell. It's very simple: *discern* and *cooperate*. God is the one who ultimately brings comfort to all of us. We can't solve other people's problems and we can't give them peace. But we *can* minister God's comfort to them by discerning what is happening in their life and by helping facilitate their cooperation with God. Now, within that framework, I'd like to suggest several guidelines for becoming a channel of God's comfort to those in pain.

Becoming an Instrument of Healing

To be a truly useful instrument of healing in God's hands:

1. *Never compromise on sin*

It's important to call sin what God calls it. Don't back off from describing the works of the flesh in the same terms the Bible uses. In Galatians 5:19-21 the apostle Paul uses strong words to describe ungodly actions: selfishness, jealousy, anger, sexual immorality, idolatry, witchcraft, hatred, discord, envy, drunkenness. Paul took sin seriously, and that's why he wrote in Galatians 5:21, "I warn you, as I did before, that those who live like this will not inherit the kingdom of God." Remember, Paul was writing these words to believers, just as he wrote 1 Corinthians 6:9-10 and Ephesians 5:5 for believers. We should always take God's side against sin.

We must be careful not to be "taken in" by a person's hurts or allow ourselves to be so overwhelmed by the difficulty of their painful circumstances that we excuse their behavior. Sometimes, in an effort to be compassionate, I think we actually try to be more gracious than God. Yet there is a time for firmness; this, too, is an expression of love. If we fail to love people in this way and excuse them from their wrong responses, they will not come into healing.

Certainly it's important for us to enter into other people's pain and empathize with what they're going through. We shouldn't preach at them when we talk to them. But we must recognize that God does hold even the most wounded person responsible for his actions. We can see this in the life of Michal and her father, Saul.

Never was there a more problem-ridden family than this one, and never was there a biblical example of a man who made more excuses for his sin than Saul.

In 1 Samuel 13:11-12, Saul offered an unauthorized sacrifice and then blamed it on his own men and Samuel: "When I saw that the men were scattering, and that you did not come at the set time...I felt compelled to offer the burnt offering."

Later on, when Saul disobeyed God's command to totally destroy his enemies and instead saved some of the best plunder, he blamed it on his soldiers: "The soldiers brought them from the Amalekites; they spared the best of the sheep and cattle to sacrifice to the LORD your God, but we totally destroyed the rest....The soldiers took sheep and cattle from the plunder, the best of what was devoted to God, in order to sacrifice them to the LORD your God at Gilgal."

Here was a tall, handsome man (1 Samuel 9:2) riddled with deep feelings of insecurity and self-consciousness. He was a man given to fits of rage (1 Samuel 19:9-10; 20:33; 22:17) and extreme jealousy (1 Samuel 18:8-9). In a word, he was emotionally unstable. Saul's daughter Michal was reared in this horrible environment, yet God held both Saul and Michal responsible for their choices. Michal was held responsible. . . .

+ though she was reared in this painful environment;

+ though she was handed off like a prize to David for killing Philistines (1 Samuel 18:27);

+ though David abandoned her when he fled from Jerusalem (1 Samuel 19:11-13);

+ though David did not go right back to her when he returned, but sent an emissary to collect her and force her to come back. During his absence Michal had remarried, and in one of the sadder scenes in the Bible, her new husband, Paltiel, follows behind weeping as she is being forcefully dragged off to be reunited with David (2 Samuel 3:12-16).

Michal—hurt, bitter, feeling abandoned, and perhaps unable to put words to her deep feelings—becomes critical of David . . . and God holds her responsible for it (2 Samuel 6:20-23). The Bible says she "had no children to the day of her death" (verse 23).

Please don't think that I'm minimizing the importance of showing compassion. Showing compassion is a given. But I do want to emphasize this point: We cannot compromise on sin because God holds us responsible for our actions and responses. We have to name sin for what it is. Always take God's side against sin.

2. *Listen wisely*

It's essential to hear all sides of an issue. On more than one occasion I have been taken in by a wounded, weeping person who described how horrible somebody else was. On those occasions when I've gone back and double-checked the facts in question, I have often found that the wounded person grossly exaggerated or sometimes just imagined what other people had thought, felt, or done to them. At times there *was* true woundedness, but I had so taken up the offense of the person that I lost my objectivity. When you are listening to a wounded person, it is important to remember there is another side to the story.

As you listen, ask righteous questions, not slanderous ones. Don't ask questions that reinforce judgment on another person. Let your questions be neutral, balanced, and open-ended. Ask "What," "why," "when," and "how" questions. Don't load your questions like a courtroom lawyer who points his finger at the witness on the stand and says, "Is it not true that when you encountered this gentleman—my client—that you were pointing an umbrella at him? Just answer the question, yes or no. And is it not true that there was a metal tip on the end of your umbrella? Just answer the question, sir, yes or no. And is it not true, sir, that my dear client was feeling attacked by you? Just answer the question, yes or no. So sir, is it not possible that my client felt it was necessary to defend himself from you—all six feet and six inches of you, who was attacking my client with your pointed-tip umbrella?"

If there seems to be a ring of authenticity to the courtroom scenario I just described, that's because such an incident really did happen to me. A number of years ago I happened upon a thief who had broken into the office where I worked. I grabbed an umbrella to defend myself and pointed it at the thief, who was standing a short distance away with a knife in his hand. He looked at me, started to dart at me, and I said, "Go! I don't want anything from you. Get out!" The thief ran out the door and into the arms of the policemen who had just arrived. Later I was called to testify at the man's trial, and the defense lawyer put me on the stand and tried to make *me* look like I had attempted to attack the thief!

It is important for us to be careful to listen righteously. Don't ask yes or no questions that set up another person to be the cause of all the problems. "You mean your father beat you?" "Did this happen to you more than once?" "Did it happen to your father's father? It must have happened to your father's father's father." Instead, ask questions like, "What were the circumstances?" "How do you feel about it?" "How have you responded?" "What are your struggles?"

You will also want to be careful not to ask questions that call the person to evaluate the motives of another person. We can never know another person's motives; such questions can lead us to be judgmental. The purpose in asking questions is to get the facts and to help the person identify his emotions and ascertain his response.

At some point you will need to ask the person to

consider what God's response might be: "How has God been dealing with you about this?" "What responses do you feel God wants you to make?" "What have you been learning from God's Word?" "How have others counseled you to respond in this situation or to this person?" "What lessons are you learning from what you have gone through?" "What would you do differently next time?"

3. Don't try to be God for other people; you're not qualified for the job

There are certain things God can do in a person's life that we cannot do. If we try to take responsibility for what only God can do, we will fail miserably. Beyond that, we will encourage people to depend upon us instead of upon the Lord.

Your responsibility is to hear a person's hurt, take it seriously, give him hope, and then assist him as he looks to God and what He says in His Word. As he listens, receives, and acts upon that, he will grow into a healthy dependence upon the Lord Himself and not upon you.

Remember, God already has been at work in the life of every person who comes to us with a need. God worked in his life before you met him, God is working in his life as you minister to him, and God will continue to work in his life even if you have no further contact with him.

As you work with a person in pain, be sensitive to the possibility that you can be manipulated by him. I learned a long time ago never to take responsibility for another person's actions. I have to remind myself of that whenever I talk to people who have suicidal urges or inclinations.

The ultimate act of manipulation is, "If you don't help me, I will kill myself." I have had to look a person in the eyes and say, "If you do that, that's your choice. I'm not responsible. I don't want you to kill yourself and I hope you don't. I would like to help you. But killing yourself is your choice, and it won't solve any of your problems."

Counselors advise that when you're talking to a suicidal person you should take him seriously and tell him that. Ask him how much he has thought about suicide. Has he attempted it? Then offer to get him professional help. Some of the people I've counseled have actually gone ahead and tried to take their life. In one situation, a person did succeed in taking his own life. But we are not responsible for such a choice. We can do only what we can do; we are not God for other people.

A counselor once warned me, "Floyd, don't say to a person, '*We* will overcome this suicidal tendency,' because then you're saying that you have taken responsibility for that person's choices along with him. You cannot do that. All you can say is, 'I will help you, but you can do it. You can overcome this situation.'"

We are not God. We are to willingly accept the responsibility to encourage and help people, but we must let them take responsibility for their choices.

4. *Create an environment of grace and truth*

The apostle John wrote these words about Jesus: "From the fullness of his grace we have all received one blessing after another. For the law was given through Moses; grace and truth came through Jesus Christ" (John 1:16-17).

We are not the source of grace and truth, but we can help create an environment where people can receive grace and truth from Jesus Christ. We need to convince people that even though they make mistakes they have the freedom to learn, to ask questions, to disagree, and to express their emotions and their feelings honestly. When we give people the freedom to be honest with themselves, with one another and with God, then they're in a prime position to receive the grace that God wants to give them and to be confronted by the truth that God brings through Jesus Christ. Confrontation can provide security for a person if it is done lovingly and honestly.

To truly love people is not merely to give them lots of warm hugs and fuzzy feelings. At times, true love requires that we sit down and talk honestly about consequences. I've often had to say to a person, "What you said has hurt me. If you keep hurting me, I won't want to be around you." By saying that, I'm trying to help that person take responsibility for his choices and recognize that other people have feelings as well. In doing that, I'm lovingly and relationally confronting the person. I try to do this in a way that shows the person our friendship is not at risk, but he *can* count on me to be both accepting and honest with him.

At our training institute in Colorado, I run an internship program for people under the age of 30 who have leadership potential. Over and over again these candidates have said to me, "Please give me feedback. Tell me how I'm doing. Coach me. I want to know how to grow in my leadership skills."

I have found that when I'm honest with the young person, when I not only encourage him or her but also say, "I think I can help you to improve what you're doing in leading the team (or planning the weekend outreach, or leading the Bible study, or overseeing the worship service)," that person loves it. I'm the same way. I like it when people give me honest, constructive input about how I can grow or improve. Doing this lovingly and honestly creates a lot of security and helps us grow.

Recently I spoke with one of the interns I'm working with. He was using a lot of "spiritual slang"—he would add a lot of "hallelujahs," "praise the Lords," and "glory to Gods" into his conversations. I shocked him one day when I said, "Harry, I'm struggling a little with your swearing."

"What do you mean?" he said, alarmed.

"Well," I replied, "you're using a lot of Christian swear words." I smiled at him and though he was confused, he could see that I was trying to communicate something.

"Please tell me what you mean," he said.

"Well, you use words a lot that I'm not really sure you mean. They are important words, like "hallelujah" and "glory" and "praise the Lord," but you use them so often—when you're nervous, when you're excited, when you're emphatic about something you're saying—I just wonder if you really mean them all the time. In fact, I think it's turning off some people and would be especially frustrating to some non-Christians."

He nodded his head slowly and replied, "You know, I think you're right."

Since then, I've noticed his conversation has changed dramatically. I made sure he knew I was not offended by him or put off, but that I was committed to him as a friend. That kind of feedback is essential for us as brothers and sisters in Christ if we're going to grow together.

5. Get professional help if you're in over your head

I often call friends who are counselors to ask for advice or for a referral when I realize I don't have the time or skills to assist someone who comes to me for help. Keep handy a good resource list of counselors who are godly, principled people. Then when somebody comes to you with a problem too complex for you to handle, you'll have the name of a competent professional you can recommend with confidence.

6. Never underestimate the "God factor"!

When we help people with problems—whether it be divorce, conflict in relationships, alcoholism, physical or verbal abuse, or anything else—we can sometimes get so overwhelmed that we forget God can redeem the worst of situations. He redeemed a murderer named Moses, an adulterer named David, and a persecutor

KISS THE TALKING FROG

named Paul—He has even saved you and me! That should give us great hope for others.

An acquaintance of mine was driving down the highway complaining to the Lord because people had been criticizing him. "Lord," he said, "they're even lying about me." Quick as a flash, he said the Lord seemed to reply in his mind, "My son, just be glad they don't know the truth about you."

God has forgiven us of all of our sins. He can forgive *anybody* and redeem *any* situation.

One of my dearest friends is a man named John Goodfellow. A book titled *Streetwise* has been written about John's past as a thief, violent gang member, alcoholic, and young man with a terrible, uncontrollable temper.

Many years ago John came to us because a cute, 19-year-old girl showed interest in him. She invited him for a meal to our outreach center. He was impressed with this girl so he went along.

To make a long story short, John accepted Christ and went back to Nottingham, England, to face the criminal charges against him. He spent two years paying off debts after the court put him on probation, led 80 friends to the Lord during those two years, started a small Bible study that grew into a church, returned to Amsterdam to join us, married a wonderful young woman from the United States, and today is an evangelist who has traveled all over the world to preach the gospel. John just took two years off to attend Columbia International University (formerly Columbia Bible School) where he completed studies toward his Master's degree. John told me in his distinct British accent, "Floyd, I never thought there would be a day when *I* would be studying theology. Can you imagine—me, a street thief, now a seminary graduate!"

There is no way to overstate the importance of the God factor. A lot of people believe that God doesn't care. They think He took a hike when they went through their hard time—that He vacated, took off, left them, abandoned them. Or they imagine that He is not at work seeking to redeem the painful situations in their life. If we are to help such people, we need to ask ourselves if we really believe God loves this person more than we do and is more committed to him or her than we are?

For more than 30 years I have been helping people in pain—everybody from drug addicts and prostitutes to burned-out spiritual leaders. I have seen many people healed by the power of God's love without ever recognizing why they were hurt or who hurt them. I've seen them respond with deep gratefulness to God's love and take responsibility for their lives. In that very moment when they accepted God's love and owned up to how they had responded to others, an amazing transformation took place. A new dignity graced their life. They found that they had the power to respond to other people in ways unimaginable before.

That's the God factor, and we should never underestimate it. It saved John Goodfellow, and it saved you, too!

Pain Is Not a Spectator Sport

An elderly man was taking his evening walk. He was enjoying the crisp night air and the sound of the wind blowing through the trees when suddenly he heard a voice calling, "Help me, help me!" The man looked all around and saw no one, so he continued his walk. Again he heard this little voice, sounding very faint and tiny and far away: "Help me, help me!"

This time the man looked down and saw a small frog looking up at him. The frog cried out again, "Help me, help me!" The man gently lifted the frog and looked at it intently. The frog spoke. "I'm really a beautiful young princess. If you will kiss me, I will turn back into a princess and I will love you forever."

The elderly man thought for a moment, placed the frog in his big coat pocket, and continued walking. The confused little frog gazed up out of the pocket and cried, "Why don't you kiss me?" The old man responded, "Frankly, at this stage of my life, I would rather have a talking frog."[3]

The pain and hurt in other people's lives are not for our curiosity or speculation. God has called us to enter into that pain—to kiss the frog and get emotionally involved. We serve a loving God "who comforts us in all our troubles, so that we can comfort those in any trouble with the comfort we ourselves have received from God" (2 Corinthians 1:4).

So go ahead. Kiss the frog! You might not find a princess, but you'll definitely delight the King.

Notes

Chapter 1—Pain and Its Power
1. "Snakes Are Not for Petting," *Parables, Etc.*, December 1994, vol. 14, num. 9, p. 3.

Chapter 2—If It's Pain, I Don't Want It!
1. Robert McGee, *The Search for Significance* (Houston, TX: Rapha Publishing, 1985), p. 28.
2. There is a controversy over whether these Galatians were Jewish converts from the south or Gentiles from the north. In my judgment, the latter option makes the most sense.
3. McGee, p. 165.
4. "The Beauty Remains," *The Pastor's Story File*, May 1994, vol. 10, no. 7, p. 1.

Chapter 3—Setting Our Feelings Free
1. "Too Much Comfort," *The Pastor's Story File*, November 1994, vol. 11, no. 1, p. 2.

Chapter 4—That's No Way to Get Healed!
1. "ABC Nightly News," Friday, April 8, 1994.
2. Michael Azerrad, *Come As You Are: The Story of Nirvana* (New York: Doubleday, 1994), p. 354.

    In fact, that was why Nirvana's music was so popular. Kurt Cobaine sang out of his own personal pain, and a generation of kids identified with him. They heard their own heart cry when they listened to Kurt sing. Some rock music expresses rebellion, but Nirvana's music expressed pain.

    Sadly, Kurt Cobaine was a victim of his own popularity. He never wanted to be a rock star, especially one who was idolized and who was looked to for answers to other people's pain.
3. Larry B. Stammer, "Pastor Reveals Reasons for Resignation," *The Los Angeles Times*, February 20, 1993, p. B1.
4. "Needs and Idols," *Christianity Today*, May 16, 1994, p. 21.
5. Karen S. Peterson, "Is society searching for quick-fix psychotherapy?" *The Desert Sun*, November 26, 1994, p. C5.
6. Robert McGee, *The Search for Significance* (Houston, TX: Rapha Publishing, 1985).

Chapter 5—God's Own Pain
1. Tim Kimmel, *Little House on the Freeway* (Portland, OR: Multnomah Press, 1987), pp. 56-59.
2. *The New Bible Commentary: Revised*, ed. D. Guthrie, J.A. Motyer and others (Grand Rapids, MI: Eerdmans Publishing Co., 1970), p. 714.
3. See Isaiah 57:15 (KJV).
4. See 2 Peter 3:8; also Psalm 90:4.
5. "Stenagmos" in William F. Arndt and F. Wilbur Gingrich, *A Greek-English Lexicon of the New Testament and Other Early Christian Literature* (Chicago: University of Chicago Press, 1979), p. 766.
6. "Groan," *The Random House College Dictionary, Revised Edition* (New York: Random House, 1988), p. 582.
7. C.J. Ellicott, *A New Testament Commentary for English Readers* (New York: E.P. Dutton, n.d.), p. 238.

8. "Fauvism and Expressionism" in *The Random House Encyclopedia, New Revised Third Edition* (New York: Random House, 1990), p. 1294.

9. "Passion for Greatness," *The Pastor's Story File*, May 1994, vol. 10, no. 7, p. 3.

10. "Mirror Magic," *The Pastor's Story File*, May 1994, vol. 10, no. 7, p. 2.

Chapter 6—From My Head to My Heart

1. "Exploration," *The New Encyclopaedia Britannica*, vol. 19 (Chicago: Encyclopaedia Britannica, Inc., 1988), plates 3, 52.

2. John MacArthur, *Our Sufficiency in Christ* (Chicago: Moody Press, 1991), pp. 25-26.

3. "When God Felt Good," *Parables, Etc.*, November 1994, vol. 14, no. 9, p. 3.

Chapter 7—The Healing Power of Love

1. This illustration and many of the insights on justification as presented in this chapter are taken and adapted from a talk by Becky Pippert at the Women in Ministry seminar in Portland, Oregon, sponsored by Multnomah Bible College.

2. David Needham, *Alive for the First Time* (Sisters, OR: Multnomah Press, 1995), p. 83.

3. Needham, p. 83.

4. Needham, p. 85.

5. Needham, pp. 88, 89.

6. Needham, pp. 91, 92.

7. Peter Lord, "Turkeys & Eagles," from a church publication, n.d.

8. Lord.

9. Lord.

10. Lord.

Chapter 8—A Moment to Be Cured...

1. Peter Lord, "Turkeys & Eagles," from a church publication, n.d.

2. Lord.

3. "Fly High," *Parables, Etc.*, May 1994, vol. 14, no. 3, p. 5.

Chapter 9—Breaking the Power of Satan's Lies

1. "From Boat to Bat," *The Pastor's Story File*, May 1994, vol. 10, no. 7, p. 6.

2. Neil Anderson, "The Battle for Your Mind," *Equipping the Saints* magazine.

3. Robert McGee, *The Search for Significance* (Houston, TX: Rapha Publishing, 1985), p. 158.

4. Anderson, pp. 18-19.

5. Anderson, p. 19.

6. Anderson, p. 19.

7. John Piper, *Desiring God* (Portland, OR: Multnomah Press, 1986), p. 14.

Chapter 10—Kiss the Talking Frog

1. "Ride with Me, Sir," *Parables, Etc.*, November 1994, vol. 14, no. 9, p. 4.

2. "When Tickets Don't Hurt," *The Pastor's Story File*, May 1994, vol. 10, no. 7, p. 6.

3. "Don't Kiss the Frog," *Parables, Etc.*, May 1994, vol. 14, no. 3, p. 1.

About the Author

Floyd McClung, Jr. is the founder and director of Mission Village in Trinidad, Colorado. Mission Village is a growing community of training and outreach ministries committed to raising up a new generation of young world-changers for Jesus.

Mission Village sponsors one-year youth leadership schools, discipleship and evangelism schools, biblical studies programs, short-term outreaches, sports and outdoor adventure opportunities, drama teams, and many other exciting programs that are reaching, equipping, and mobilizing a vast army of young men and women to reach the world for Christ.

If you would like more information about how you can become part of Mission Village or attend one of the training schools offered at Mission Village, write today to:

Mission Village
P.O. Box 5
Trinidad, CO 81082
USA

Other Good Harvest House Reading

THE FATHER HEART OF GOD
by *Floyd McClung*

In a world that is confused about God and beguiled by distorted images of His nature—it's time to discover for yourself the amazing and compassionate love He offers. McClung richly illustrates how the loving, compassionate Father Heart of God enables us to overcome insecurity and the devastating effects of some of life's most painful experiences. A study guide with questions for each chapter is included.

GOD'S MAN IN THE FAMILY
by *Floyd McClung*

Complicated burdens and unrealistic expectations have made it nearly impossible for today's Christian man to keep up with his role as a husband and father. Yet God didn't design for that to happen. Join bestselling author Floyd McClung, Jr. as he shares nine rock-solid, life-tested, biblical principles that will help free a man from tangled priorities and provide him with clear direction for true fulfillment.

HEALING THE HURTING HEART
by *June Hunt*

Everyone faces trying times. This book of letter excerpts and heartfelt responses shows simply and practically how to deal with temptation, the desires of the flesh, and the enormous pressure exerted by the world in daily situations. Addressing issues from anger to jealousy to loneliness and much more, Hunt offers the only answers that can truly help—answers from God's Word.

A STILLNESS IN THE STORM
by *Anabel Gillham*

When in need of wisdom, guidance, or help, sometimes we can find great comfort in considering how God has answered the prayers of fellow believers. Anabel Gillham allows us an opportunity to do just that by sharing select portions from her prayer journal of 20-plus years. Her words are a wellspring of encouragement to anyone who yearns to find shelter in God's arms amid the stormy seas of life.